I'M POSSIBLE

Breaking limits to achieve the impossible

Yemi Oyinkansola

I'mPossible

Breaking limits to achieve the impossible

Copyright © 2020 by **Yemi Oyinkansola**

Paperback ISBN: 978-1-952098-31-4

Printed in the United States of America. All rights reserved solely by the publisher. This book or parts thereof may not be reproduced in any form, stored in a retrieval system, or transmitted in any form by any means - electronic, mechanical, photocopy. Unless otherwise noted, Bible quotations are taken from the Holy Bible, King James Version. Copyright 1982 by Thomas Nelson, Inc., publishers. Used by permission.

Published by:
Cornerstone Publishing
A Division of Cornerstone Creativity Group LLC
Info@thecornerstonepublishers.com
www.thecornerstonepublishers.com
+1 516.547.4999

Author's Contact

For speaking engagement or to order books by Pastor Yemi Oyinkansola, please send email to oyemi99@gmail.com or call +1 510.258.4583.

Dedication

I want to specially dedicate this book to my Beautiful and Lovely Daughter, **Melody Doyinsolu Ajoke Oyinkansola** for her spirit of resilience, toughness, never give up, Possibility, and strength in pursuing her passion in life. Impossibility is never in her vocabulary.

Growing up, One of the Bible Passage I made her to memorize and recite often is Philippians 4:13 .... I can do all things through Christ who strengthens me. She always believe she can do all things she put her heart to do through her Faith in Christ Jesus and that with God all things are possible.

Melody, I love your never give up spirit and I'm so proud of you. Keep soaring high with wings as Eagle into your Glorious destiny in Jesus name. The sky is never your limit...

Acknowledgments

Firsttly, I will like to acknowledge my Lord and Savior Jesus Christ for saving me and for sparing my life to see the beauty of today. I appreciate God for His unmerited grace upon me that brought the inspiration for this book.

I specially acknowledge and thank my beautiful wife Comfort and lovely children, Melody, Faithful and Toluwani for their love and support always.

I appreciate the resident Pastor of Jesus House Antioch Pastor Kayode Daniels, his wife Seun Daniels, my staff members, JHA ministers and the entire JHA family for their love and support... I love you all.

Finally, I acknowledge and appreciate Pastor Gbenga Showunmi, my able, creative, talented, professional and anointed publisher and his team at Cornerstone Creativity Group for putting this book and my thought together. More grace sir.

For all my readers, I specially appreciate you for reading through this book for knowledge and impartation to move from the realm of Impossibility to the realm where you can boldly say I am POSSIBLE come what may. Luke 1:37- For with God nothing shall be impossible.

Contents

Dedication..5
Acknowledgments..6
Introduction..9

Chapter 1
Think Possibility..13

Chapter 2
All Things Are Possible..33

Chapter 3
You Are Not The Only One....................................49

Chapter 4
Principles Of Possibility Thinking..........................63

Chapter 5
The Power Of Your Words.....................................79

Chapter 6
Make Your Life Intentional....................................93

Chapter 7
Winners Never Quit...109

Introduction

In almost every narrative of great victories and accomplishment in life, there is usually an aspect that many people are not aware of – the story of where it all actually began. From time to time, we celebrate champions, trailblazers, record-breakers and others who achieve the seemingly impossible in all facets of life; but, often, our attention is fixed on the immediate feat that is visible to all.

As you probe further, however, you will discover a universal truth about these breakthroughs: Battles are first won in the mind before they are won on the battlefield. Mountains are first crushed on the inside before they are uprooted on the outside. Success is first stamped upon the subconscious mind before it is eventually actualized for the world to see.

This is the most powerful secret you will find about every achiever, whether in the spiritual or in the physical. They first visualize their success in their minds, then live it, breathe it, speak it – till it becomes a consuming passion that drives them forward and fills them with such unfathomable passion that blinds them to the sights of barriers, deafens them to the sounds of discouragement, and fortifies them against fears till they reach their goal. Since they have conquered the greatest of all battles – the battle of the mind – they become unbreakable and unstoppable until they triumph and are celebrated.

Unfortunately, as it goes for achievers, so also it is for underachievers and those who end up as outright failures. It all begins in the mind. Usually, it is not the battles they face that consume them. It is not their physical disability, poor background, dysfunctional family, disadvantaged community or even the series of disappointments and setbacks that they experience that consume them; it is the chains with which they have shackled themselves in their minds. They see themselves as deficient and they end up being frustrated.

It is cheering however that God's desire for humanity in general and for you in particular is to succeed and not to fail; to conquer and not be conquered. And even more heartwarming is that He has made all the provisions for you to rise above difficulties and fulfil your destiny. All you need do is look beyond the seeming limitations that surround you to see the doors of opportunities and possibilities that are open wide for you to explore.

This is the very purpose of this book – to shift your gaze from the finite challenges that are seeking to hold you down, to the infinite potentials, privileges and promises that God has made available for you to enjoy all-round success in life. More importantly, you will find, in this book, such empowering revelations that will lift your spirits and inspire you to take your rightful place among the champions of destiny, who consistently turn stumbling blocks to stepping stones and discover goldmines of opportunities, even in the worst form of adversity!

1

THINK POSSIBILITY

"Nothing paralyzes our lives like the attitude that things can never change. We need to remind ourselves that God can change things. Outlook determines outcome. If we see only the problems, we will be defeated; but if we see the possibilities in the problems, we can have victory."

- Warren Wiersbe

One of the most powerful gifts you have been blessed with as a human being is your mind. That mind of yours is a powerhouse of imaginations, aspirations and innovations. Through your mind, you can see things that are yet to happen, travel through time, envision the kind of life you want for yourself, and come up with extraordinary solutions to existing problems.

Everything that has ever been created or invented was first visualized in the mind before it became a physical reality. Even the creation of the earth and its inhabitants began in the mind of God before the creative declarations were made. And it is interesting that God imagined and called out exactly what He wanted, despite the emptiness, darkness and meaninglessness that initially characterized the earth. He did not allow any of these realities to bother Him.

It goes without saying then that both the outcomes of our daily experiences and the direction of our lives, in general, are significantly determined by the contents, inclinations and direction of our mind. This is why someone said, *"You cannot feature in a future that you cannot picture."* This is apparently so because the future of hope, joy and fulfilment of dreams and expectations only belongs to those who can first picture it in their mind.

It is for this reason that I am inviting you to the life-changing world of possibility thinkers – the world of those who, as John C. Maxwell puts it, have developed the orientation to see possibilities everywhere instead of limitations. You must think possibility before you can conquer the impossible and achieve the incredible!

GEARING YOUR MIND FOR POSSIBILITIES

Your mind is a formidable component of your life that makes you a "little god" – with amazing creative power and ability. God Himself declared, **"I have said, Ye are gods; and all of you are."** (Psalm 82:6). Being a "god" automatically means that you should be above limitations and so should not see yourself as helpless, disadvantaged, confined, inferior or incapacitated. Rather, it should make you consider yourself blessed, powerful, privileged, loaded and unstoppable.

This realization should make you begin to re-examine how you have been using your mind. How have you been seeing yourself – your present circumstances and future prospects? Examine the thoughts and pictures that have been dominating your mind recently; do you see possibilities or difficulties? Do you imagine barriers or breakthroughs?

As I already stated, everything you see in the world first began in the mind. In the same way, everything that comes to your life is often a reflection of what is in your mind. This makes it imperative for you to be very selective about what your mind dwells on. It is said that your thoughts have a way of attracting a certain type of occurrence, people, and resources into your life. This is because our thoughts propel us into action, into the direction the thoughts are focused on. That is why your mind must be tuned towards possibilities.

This also indicates that the mind, to a great extent, has a firm grip on behavior. Substantiating this, Apostle Joshua Selma stated that "the physical body is an executor of what the mind dictates" Little wonder psychologists would observe human behavior to get a hint of what goes on in the mind. In other words, your behavior is a reflection of what you are thinking. That is why Scripture says *"**As he thinketh in his heart, so is he**"* (Proverbs 23:7).

For instance, if an individual thinks he is poor, weak, unfortunate, unlucky, so is he! If he thinks he is hated, not popular, will never move forward or will never achieve anything, so is he. If he sees himself as a child of God; as a favored, fortunate, happy, successful, and victorious person, so is he! That's how dominant the mind can be.

THE FOUNTAIN OF GREATNESS

It's quite interesting how many people work so hard to improve the external behavior while they ignorantly neglect the source of all actions and achievements. Armed with a perfect understanding of the human make-up, King Solomon, under the inspiration of the Holy Spirit advised, **"*Keep thy heart with all diligence; for out of it are the issues of life*"** (Proverbs 4:23). Conclusively, if you need to change your narrative, you need to begin with your mind.

Truly, the ability to think is a very unique one. One fascinating thing about the imagination is that there is no limit to what you can imagine and bring to reality in your mind. The perfect example of an imaginative mind is the Triune God. As I mentioned above, everything that was ever created started from the mind and was spoken into reality. Before speaking can take place, it has to happen first in the mind. The Bible clearly records in Genesis 1;26-27, **"*And God said, let us make man in our image, after our likeness: and let them have dominion over the fish of the sea, and over the fowl*** *of the air, and over the cattle, and over all the earth, and over every creeping thing that creepeth upon the earth. So God created man in his own image, in the image of God created he him; male and female created he them."*

God had an understanding of what He created because it had been concluded in the mind. He thought to create man differently from other creatures to till the ground and be lord over the things created; and thus making man in His image became a reality. And the Bible records that God rested on the 7th day after creating everything imagined.

A famous achiever once said, *"The man who has no imagination has no wings."* This is truly apt. A person who cannot explore his imaginations cannot go far; in fact, limitation is not far from such a person. In life, there is no end to whatever can be achieved, once you can dream and imagine it. Understanding that the mind is very powerful usually can be a motivation in itself.

A renowned speaker in Africa once revealed that when he started as a young man, he had the exact picture of how he wanted his house to be. He had a place in mind, but he wasn't buoyant enough to buy land, not to talk of building a house. He really did not know how it would come to fruition, but he understood the power of possibility thinking, backed up with diligence and discipline. Over time, he kept reaffirming what his pictured reality was and eventually, the time came to get a land. There was no land for sale at that time, but he was relentless. He kept pushing until he acquired a house in his dream area. This might seem like a small thing to others, but it was a huge achievement for him and it all started from the mind.

Wherever you see yourself in your imagination, with much work and labor you can get there. If your imaginative power is dormant, you'll remain stagnant, you cannot fly. I saw a movie recently, in which a young poor boy had a dream that one day, he would become the owner of a company. It sounded incredible because he had no means of even getting primary education, yet he didn't stop believing. His parents discouraged him and told him to stop dreaming, but he wouldn't. One day, he left home and went to a nearby school to learn at all cost, but he was chased back home. He kept on going until someone saw his willingness and agreed to sponsor him through his primary education. From there doors of opportunities opened and he became what he imagined.

Truth is, where there is a will, there will always be a way. If you can imagine it, it will surely come to pass if you are willing to pay the price. The creative power of imagination has an important role in the achievement of success in any area. As Denis Waitley says, *"You have all the reason in the world to achieve your grandest dreams. Imagination plus innovation equals realization."*

KEY TO UPLIFTING CHANGE

So far, we have established that possibility thinking is a state in which the mind is conditioned to develop and dwell on pleasant, promising, and positive imaginations and resolutions. It is a mental attitude that creates and channels your energy towards positivity.

Multitudes of compelling proofs abound – in Scripture, science, history and experience – to show that people who possess possibility mentality end up becoming successful in their careers and personal lives than people who only expect the worst from any situation or anyone. People with possibility mindset focus on the positive side of life at all times and in all circumstances. No wonder things often work out for them. This is why it has been said that *"When you are sinking, consider what you are thinking."*

Your thoughts are so powerful that they determine the course of your life. Indeed, the moment you take a decision to overhaul your thinking system, you will immediately begin to notice a change in every area of your life. So, if you want to be elevated from the level you are right now, all you need do is simply change your thoughts from negativity and impossibility to positivity and possibility. Change your thoughts, and your personality will change. Change your thoughts and victory, success, dominion, healing, and deliverance will be all yours.

Now don't get it wrong by thinking that all you need

to do is sit down idly and be imagining pleasant things without taking any actions towards accomplishment. What is being said is that positive thinking broadens your senses to see or perceive the various options open to you to achieve a particular goal. It also energizes you. To tell you the truth, nothing stimulates better than the thoughts of a positive outcome. Your thought is like a forerunner of your actions, and to some extent, your achievement.

GOD'S GOT YOUR BACK

It is also important you know the revealed thoughts of God concerning your life and align your thoughts with His. This is one important factor that will help you achieve the ultimate in life. He says, *"I know the thoughts that I think toward you, saith the LORD, thoughts of peace, and not of evil, to give you an expected end"* (Jeremiah 29:11).

Are you wondering how to know the thoughts of God concerning you in various areas of life? What God wants you to know about His thoughts and will for you are written in His Word—the Bible. Study it. As you read the Word of God regularly, you will find that you will begin to think the way God thinks about you.

He never thinks in weakness. God has never been incapacitated. He is never hindered by man or Satan in whatever He wants to do. Thus, Pharaoh could not stop Him from taking the Israelites out of Egypt. The fire of Nebuchadnezzar did not intimidate Him when He wanted to deliver Shadrach, Meshach, and Abednego. So when you think in line with the thoughts of God, you will think in terms of His power, His ability, and His promise. Think in acknowledgment of what God says He will do. It implies that you don't need to think about circumstances surrounding you or your weakness. You should rather think in relation to His power.

By thinking in acknowledgment of God's unlimited power, you will record unlimited success. You will be victorious, empowered, unconquerable, successful, and happy; for there is nothing impossible with God (Genesis 18:14). Think in line with the promise and prophecy of God's Word. God has promised abundant supply (2King7:1). Believe and think on it instead of being doubtful. Align your thought with the power and promise of God in all things. The Scripture says in Job 36:5, 11 that *"God is mighty ... If they obey and serve him, they shall spend their days in prosperity, and their years in pleasures."* Think in consideration of God's ability and divine power. For *"I know that thou canst do everything, and that no thought can be withholden from thee"* (Job 42:2). That is how to think. He made the heavens and the earth and there is nothing too hard for Him. When you face a new situation or a new challenge, it is your thought that either makes you a victor or a victim, your thoughts determine if you will have dominion, or experience defeat. That is why you need to change your thoughts. For *"with God all things are possible"* (Matthew 19:26). Think on the guaranteed possibilities in God in all spheres and challenges of life.

When your thinking is based on the power of God, you don't give up on your plans even when it appears humanly impossible. You will not be limited by your thoughts due to age or health considerations. Earthly experts might have written you off because of a particular situation, but there is no limitation with the power of God. Exercise faith in God and there *"shall be a performance of those things which were told [you] from the Lord"* (Luke1:45). Just think of God as your helper, healer, deliverer, redeemer, and your guide in decision making; for nothing is impossible with Him.

Negative thinking is dangerous and must be discarded in its entirety. It leaves you depressed and frustrated. It robs you of the mental energy to think productively. Negative thoughts can lead to emotional degeneration. It narrows your senses and makes you focus on the problem, instead of the possibilities. You may discover that instead of looking for a possible solution to a problem, you will rather waste your energy in being upset and despaired. It can make you restless and uncoordinated. Even your body system could be affected because you can fall sick as a result of depression and frustration. All these are evidence that there is nothing good about negative thinking. As such, you must eject every negative thought from your mind, so as to maximize the potentials of the power of your mind.

ATTRIBUTES OF A POSSIBILITY THINKER

Possibility thinkers are super-achievers and are known by the following attributes:

- Purpose-driven
- Not confined or paralyzed by thoughts of failure
- Seeing opportunities in adversities
- Passionate and unstoppable
- Supportive and sacrificing
- Determined and persevering
- Focused and forward-looking

A possibility thinker is driven by purpose. There is something strong and empowering from within that keeps him going even in the face of strong opposition. He is driven by the need to serve and do something not just for himself, but for others. Having a sense of purpose simply means to find something significant or dear to the heart and hold on strongly to it. No one ever achieves something great without a sense of purpose—the need to do something, a big picture. I tell you, when one is on the verge of giving up and he remembers the big picture, strength is renewed and energy refueled to continue the process.

A possibility thinker is never afraid of failure. In fact, failure is seen as a stepping stone to success. Failure is a factor for success to happen. It is no news that nothing good comes easy. It will sometimes have to take the extra effort, the many failures, before a person can attain real success in any area of life. One recurrent feature in the stories of great men is the number of times they failed before they eventually pulled through. Thomas Edison relates to this, he said, *"many of life's failures are people who did not realize how close they were to success when they gave up."* The most important factor wasn't the number of times he failed, but the one time he succeeded. I like to say that truly; failure prepares one for success in any area of life. Truth is, a possibility thinker doesn't quit at the failure stage, instead, he learns the lesson needed and proceeds until success is attained.

A possibility thinker sees an opportunity in every adversity; he doesn't believe negativity, impossibility or pessimism. The Bible gives a perfect picture of people who exemplified this attribute. In the Old Testament, an account was given in the book of Joshua. Moses had picked twelve strong men to go search the land of Canaan. On returning, ten persons out of the twelve were naysayers, they didn't see the need to continue and possess the land because they were as grasshoppers, despite agreeing that the land was flowing with milk and honey, they resorted to believing that the obstacle was larger than what could be handled. However, Joshua and Caleb were possibility thinkers. They saw beyond the obstacles and knew they could have the land. Numbers 13:30 says, *"And Caleb stilled the people before Moses, and said, let us go up at once, and possess it; for we are well able to overcome it."* The power of those two prevailed over that of the ten and eventually, despite the obstacles, the children of Israel made it to the promise land.

Passion is an outstanding quality of a possibility thinker. He has unrelenting energy with which he pursues a set goal. He isn't in the category of people who just learn to survive through life; he goes beyond his struggles to live life to the fullest. A passionate person does not leave any stone unturned, he'll rather give in everything he has to bring something to fruition. Mother Theresa is an example of a passionate human. The Catholic nun at that time defied all orders to help the helpless. She saw a need and wanted to help as many people as she can, she had a burning sense of purpose and she was passionate about it. Despite the ridicule and misunderstanding, she achieved her aim, and today, she is remembered for her good deeds around the world. A passionate person makes time for personal growth and development. Also, making sacrifices is never from a possibility thinker, due to how passionate he is about something, he'll burn the midnight candle to get it done and until it is done, he would not settle down.

Possibility thinkers are determined and persevering. Show me a man who cannot persevere and I'll show you a man who isn't ready to achieve anything. As they say, nothing good comes easy, there is always a price to pay. Benjamin Disreali said, *"through perseverance many people win success out of what seemed destined to be certain failure."* I'll explain this as the ability to keep going despite the failures, eventually winning is sure. The ability to keep pursuing a particular goal even when others abandon it is what I call perseverance. A possibility thinker is willing to hang on. He understands that there will be setbacks, delays and several crossroads. However, it is at this time that he becomes even more courageous; he is prepared go through the roller coaster process till there is light at the end of the tunnel. To be an achiever or someone of immense value, you have to possess this attribute.

Understanding the power of self-sacrifice, support and teamwork is an attribute of an achiever. A selfish person is never a possibility thinker. If in your mind, you are only after what you have to benefit, then you're a long way from making anything come to fruition. Oftentimes, it takes the joint effort of different persons to bring a vision to accomplishment. Understanding that is very important for anything to be possible. A person cannot afford to be so rigid and expect to achieve a task tagged as impossible.

Having a mind-set that incorporates others helps a person to go far in his pursuit. Allow others to share their opinion and views, give room for constructive criticism, and appreciate the effort of a team. These will help improve the quality of anything. As I said earlier, it all begins with the mind. There needs to be a reorientation that one cannot do everything by oneself, the ideas of other persons help a lot too. Teamwork is a necessity.

It is important to note that a possibility thinker has a grip on what he allows into his mind, it helps to keep him focused and avoid every unnecessary distraction. The mind is very powerful; what goes on in the mind can either make or mar a person. The possibility thinker, therefore, filters the things he dwells on. He screens out negativity as much as possible.

Attributes of an Impossibility Thinker

- Negativity and excuse-giving
- Self-imposed limitations
- Unwillingness to quit the comfort zone and take constructive risks
- Shackled by fear of the unknown
- Confessions of defeat and despair

An impossibility thinker is someone who believes that something cannot be done. It is the mentality of "I cannot". The impossibility thinker always has an excuse for why something can't be done or why it should not be done.

Unlike a possibility thinker, he'll rather stay on the safe side than sail through the rough tide. Such a mindset is fixed on only what can be physically seen. A limitation is often placed on the mind and as a result, such a person wouldn't think or do something termed impossible, he'll rather stick with the ordinary. Such a person spews negativity all around.

An impossibility thinker is always scared of taking risks. He'll rather consider the reasons why he should embark on something. The reasons keep mounting until it becomes impossible in the mind. The fear of taking risks is a bad state of mind to be in, it inhibits growths and causes huge limitations in a person's life. Moses' lifestyle at the initial stage was that of a naysayer until God worked on him. God wanted Moses to go back to Egypt and talk to Pharaoh to let His people go. Moses initially saw that as a great risk, remembering that he fled Egypt because his life was at stake. At that moment, he was in his comfort zone and was scared of going back to his actual reality. He kept giving God reasons why he couldn't do what was expected of him. After much back and forth, God allowed Aaron to be his mouthpiece. The essence of this example is not to diminish or misrepresent Moses as God eventually worked through him greatly. It's just to highlight that a naysayer is always afraid of taking risks.

Understanding that life is a risk and comes with its rough areas is a step towards coming out of the impossibility zone. Beyond that, learning to take the first step is key to facing any risk. Also, understanding that sometimes, failure is inevitable, but it shouldn't stop you from pursuing your goal. This understanding takes a naysayer to the realm of a possibility thinker.

The Old Testament records the case of Nehemiah; he saw the need for the temple at Jerusalem to be built again. He was unrelenting in pursuing the request and it was granted. Sanballat and his friends were naysayers, but Nehemiah had the mind of God, he would not allow the sayings or opposition of men to hinder the will of God. Eventually, he took a strong risk in the face of opposition, backed up with prayers, and the temple was built again.

The impossibility thinker is constantly afraid of the unknown. He hasn't taken a step, but he already sees failure at the end. He is never optimistic about life; he is rather pessimistic. A man who is constantly afraid may never set out to do anything worthwhile.

While it is okay to be afraid, the fear should be a positive drive to achieve something, not a reason not to. The ability to do things, despite being afraid, makes all the difference. Truth is, there always will be one reason or the other to be afraid, but that shouldn't be a stumbling block. Peter, a disciple of Jesus saw his master walking on water, which ordinarily would have been tagged impossible. He placed his fears aside and called out to Jesus, and he was asked to come. At that moment, he looked beyond impossibility, his mind saw the task as a possible one and he did walk on water. He only began to sink when he became afraid and took his eyes off his goal, Christ.

The words "I cannot" and "No" are not far away from the impossibility thinker. There is always a reason to say No, without even putting in the effort. The success mentality only says no to negativity; therefore, success is far away from people who only see the reason why something shouldn't be done. Sometimes, it is necessary to say no for the right reasons, maybe to a negative idea, not necessarily an opposing idea. An opposing idea can sometimes be of benefit. Oftentimes, when you hear I cannot, it is usually followed with not doing something. Sayings like, "I cannot be the best" and "I can never get out this problem" are never far from an impossibility thinker. The reality is that when you say I cannot, you never will because the mind has been programmed to believe that you cannot; but when you say you can, then you will.

Mike Norton says, "never say that you can't do something, or that something seems impossible, or that something can't be done, no matter how discouraging or harrowing it may be; human beings are limited only by what we allow ourselves to be limited by—our own minds. We are each the masters of our reality; when we become self-aware of this: absolutely anything in the world is possible."

You Are What You Think

As I round off this chapter, I feel the need to reinforce the importance of thinking possibilities. Without any doubt, we are products of what goes on in our minds. Before a word is spoken, there is first a thinking pattern. Romans 12: 2 says, *"And be not conformed to this world: but be ye transformed by the renewing of your mind, that ye may prove what is that good, and acceptable, and perfect, will of God."* The

Bible enjoins that a believer should renew his mind to be transformed.

Understanding the power of the mind and thoughts, helps you filter unnecessary information or thoughts that stray into the mind unawares. You have to guard the things that come to mind by paying extra attention to the things you do and watch; the songs you sing, and places you go to. Sometimes, a negative thought flows through the mind as a result of a book, song, or movie. Truly, some things are beyond control, but controlling the things that can be controlled saves the mind from straying and helps one to stay on course.

Discipline your mind to think positively; to see the good in every situation and look on the brighter side of every happening. It takes discipline and diligence to bring your imagination to actualization. This is because, beyond thinking, it takes action to be something. So, think big and take immediate action on your thought. Thinking without action leaves you with no achievement, you just remain on the same spot. It is like a man who dreamed and saw himself in a huge apartment, swimming in wealth, he wakes up and tells everyone around him that he is a rich man, yet goes back to his bed to sleep all day. I tell you, that man will die in penury.

Never forget, you are what you think, and you are permitted to explore your mind and speak what you want into reality, beyond speaking, learn to take action always. Remember, with God all things are possible.

2

ALL THINGS ARE POSSIBLE

"If you think something is impossible, you will block yourself from creating it - deciding possibilities is not your job!"

- A.D Largie

Life is laced with difficult and mind-boggling circumstances that constantly challenge our belief in a world of possibilities. And, perhaps, for this reason, you ask, "Is there a life of absolute and unimaginable possibilities; one without hurdles in its tracks nor clouds in its skies; a life where you are free to dream BIG even in the face of seemingly difficult oppositions without the fear of being tagged fanatical or unrealistic? A life where all things are possible?" Certainly Yes!

Let me quickly share this story with you. When he was 26, a music composer, Ludwig van Beethoven, began to lose his hearing. But this circumstance didn't prevent him from composing. When he had almost completely lost his hearing, he wrote the *Moonlight Sonata*; and even after becoming deaf, he still wrote a short piece, named *Fur Elise* (which we often hear coming from music boxes).

Thanks to his talent and strong will, Beethoven learned to listen to the music inside him. He wrote *Symphony No. 9*, and conducted the concert himself. After a triumphant performance, he started crying. He went on to make that famous statement that "there are no barriers for a person with talent and love towards work."

Possibilities, despite Difficulties

May I say to you that, as the above illustration shows, a life of "all possibilities" is only on the other side of "all difficulties"; it is not without confrontations.

Interestingly, the first mention of this phrase – "All things are possible" - was made by Jesus in the Bible. In Matthew 19, He revealed to His Disciples and others the difficulty of entering into the kingdom of God: ***"It is easier for a camel to go through the eye of a needle, than for a rich man to enter into the kingdom of God."*** Just as any normal person would respond to such a revelation, the disciples ***"were exceedingly amazed saying who then can be saved?"*** They were pondering, *with this stringent condition, it must be impossible for anyone to enter into the kingdom of God.* But just at the climax of a situation that seemed like a cul-de-sac, Jesus uttered a yet more startling phrase: *"...all things are possible."*

This short narrative brings to the fore an important lesson you may have observed: **great possibilities are birthed in the face of hopeless and daunting situations** Isn't that a paradox? It was amid great hardship and ridicule that the first practical electric light bulb was invented. A British Parliament Committee noted in 1878 that Edison's light bulb was *"good enough for our Transatlantic friends ... but unworthy of the attention of practical or scientific men."* Similarly, a chief engineer for the British Post Office said that the *"subdivision of the electric light is an absolute ignis fatuus."* In other words, a fairy tale. A sham.

Thomas Edison, later speaking on possibility, said, *"Nearly every man who develops an idea works it up to the point where it looks impossible, and then some get discouraged. That's not the place to become discouraged."* For all things are possible!

Why All Things?

I almost hear you say, "Does this actually mean ALL THINGS?" What do you think? Remember it all depends on how you see it. In life, **what** you see is important, but **how** you see is more important. Many only pay attention to what they see and not how they see. How you see what you see will determine what you will get from what you see. Yes! Sounds weird right? But it is true! What you see forms your knowledge but how you see informs your attitude towards what you see.

All things are possible literally means ALL THINGS are possible. These words could have never been plainer than that. All things simply mean the entire set of what the eyes can see as well as what the mind can ever conceive, as far as possible, without an iota of skepticism.

You've got dreams? If yes, then know that those dreams, in all their dimensions, projections and ramifications are valid. There has never been and will never be a dream or idea too large or big to be fulfilled or accomplished. The only legal institution that has the ultimate capacity to make your dreams short of "all things" is your mind. Yes, your mind!

Your mind, as has been repeatedly emphasized, has to be consciously and deliberately trained to conceive, comprehend and come to terms with the possibility of "all things" because it is in it (the mind) that your dreams must first be executed and celebrated.

Many 'great dreamers' there are who were known for nothing more than the dreams they had. They never went on to accomplish them. This is because when they were faced with challenges, they carried a mind that doubted the possibility of achieving their desires. They didn't see that 'all things', no matter how big their dreams were, are possible.

All things! Can you please pause for a second to think about it? How high, deep, or wide can you imagine? "As far as my finances, career, health, and probably my faith," I can almost seem to hear you whisper. However far, I want you to know that it's much more than all you can fathom.

This reminds me of the account of Abraham in Genesis 15:5. There, God was painting on a gigantic canvass the picture of 'all things' before the eyes of that old patriarch when *"He brought him forth abroad, and said, Look now toward heaven, and tell the stars, if thou be able to number them: and He said unto him, So shall thy seed be."*

"Whoa!" Abraham must have exclaimed in utter wonder. You will observe that an impossible but striking task was given to Abraham by God in that text, *"...Look now toward heaven, and tell the stars if thou be able to number them."* That's 'all things' right there. God knew that Abraham couldn't even attempt to number the stars but yet He put it to him.

But why? This has always been God's way of bringing us into His world of infinite possibilities. Abraham, in verse 3 of that chapter, poured out his heart to God about his need of a child, saying, *'...behold to me thou hast given no seed...'* but God's response to him, that cold starry night, in the fifth verse bout the innumerability of his seed must have been staggeringly impossible to him. He asked and hoped for one but God promised and gave him all. All things!

Is your dream small? Why not enlarge it? Oh, you say, "I will be tagged unrealistic and outrageous." So be it! Who cares? As long as your 'outrageous' dream accommodates 'all things' you've taken an important step forward towards the actualization of that dream because in a matter of time you will be celebrated.

In 2 Peter 1:3, the apostle Peter, through divine inspiration, sheds light on the definition of 'all things.' He broadens the scope of this phrase and drives it home: *"According as his divine power hath given unto us ALL THINGS that pertain to life and godliness."* This, already, is hope for you as you can see. God is so much interested in the accomplishment of your wildest dreams and aspirations. And that's why He has given you ALL THINGS without reservation. What a gift! The gift of all possibilities!

This leaves no one with the excuse of not dreaming, so, dream on, your dreams are valid, for in God's economy of ALL THINGS, the possibilities of your dreams and desires have been catered for.

Beyond Physical Limitations

Living a life of possibilities and impacts has nothing to do with your looks, stamina or stature. It has nothing to do with your race, family background, circumstances of birth, environment, nationality or connections. In fact, it is never about you in your natural self. It is about the power of God in you. *"But Jesus beheld them and said unto them, with men this is impossible, but with God all things are possible"* (Matthew 19:26).

What this means is that, in the equation of possibilities, God has never been a variable but an eternal constant. Look closely again, and you will realize that the passage above is punctuated, or better put, divided into two by the word "but." The Spirit of God, by this, evidently intends to change our line of thought, and interestingly, in the opposite direction.

The first part of the passage is quite relatable and represents the day-to-day experience of the common, unaided man—Impossibilities. Jesus said "with men," meaning that everyone in this category is implicated, including you. Limitation is an integral part of humanity; and much truer is the fact that no matter how good-willed and 'capable' any of us might seem to be, there are certain circumstances that are conveniently beyond the scope of our possibilities.

Thankfully, however, the second part of the passage reminds us of what we said earlier in this chapter about the verdict of hope. As you can observe, the phrase 'with God' changes the narrative. It is as though I see a huge beam of light finally brightening a room that had been dark for centuries; or as if I see the green leaves of a beautiful plant springing up with life and energy from the reddish-brown soil of desert at the scent of water; or as though I see the prison doors of a once-convicted criminal, who is now acquitted and discharged, swinging wide open after many years of hopeless incarceration. He now walks the streets of the city breathing the air of freedom and shouting on top of his lungs: "With God!"

John C. Maxwell, in his book titled *Be All You Can Be*, noted: *"Plan ahead, chart your course, and if God is going to be your partner, make your plans large."* Hello, there is no situation hopeless, mountain insurmountable, project unworkable, or dream unachievable with God!

Imperative of Divine Partnership

The phrase, "with God" leaves us with the imperative of partnership. Your dreams, no matter how lofty or little, are not more than mere dreams without God. It is only with God that all things are possible. Antecedents have furnished us with a plethora of accounts of men and women; ordinary people who went on to dare the impossible all in the strength of their partnership with God and had their names etched into our minds and hearts.

Nick Vujicic, the man born without arms and legs, made an astounding statement on partnership with God. He said, *"I don't need arms and legs; I just need Him."* This maxim helped him to become one of the most famous motivational speakers, receive an economics degree, get married, and have two children. In his book titled *Your Life Without Limits*, Nick told how the words of his mother set the tone for a lifetime. "*Nicholas*," she said, *"you need to play with normal children because you are normal.*

You just have a few bits and pieces missing, that's all."

Jesus, teaching his disciples on the onus of partnership, beautifully revealed in the book of John 15:4 in a fashion that demands every inch of reflection: *"For without me ye can do nothing."* It is with Him that all things are possible. Similarly, but in a stronger tone, Jesus, in the book of Mark 10:27, zeroes in on the rationale behind divine-human partnership in the achievement of your dreams and goals – God's omnipotence; *"… with men it is impossible but not with God, for with God all things are possible."* The phrase 'but not with God' should propel you to place your trust in God and stake your life's dreams on His unequalled ability.

God has proven Himself over and over again as the unending source of all resources, and I mean ALL. He longs for your partnership because you are only better off 'with' Him. The nuances of your dream's peculiarity, the resources for its actualization as well as the roadmap to its destination are with Him. He's worthy of your partnership for with Him there's no disappointment.

Of this David said in Psalms 18:29, *"For by thee I have run through a troop and by my God have I leaped over a wall."*

To Him that Believeth

It is in the ninth chapter of the Gospel according to Mark that this account was narrated. A true story. It begins from the seventeenth verse where "*one of the multitude answered and said Master, I have brought unto thee my son, which hat a dumb spirit…and I spake to thy disciples that they should cast him out and they could not."*

Before the gazing audience of skeptics, Jesus replied the father of the sick child with a statement that showed His disappointment in His disciples but quite instructive for us: *"He answereth him, and saith, O faithless generation…"* If you intently followed this account to this point, you'll probably perceive the feeling of deep displeasure apparent in the comment of Jesus. He named that generation faithless. Definitely, He least expected such a degree of faithlessness in God from a generation that has witnessed a barrage of miracles.

In short, Jesus was drawing their attention to the excellence of faith as well as the tragedy of its absence, especially in the face of an 'impossible' situation like this. Do you think faith is crucial to the possibility of your dreams or you think you've got your plans all figured out on your own? Are you presently in the valley of broken dreams and think faith in God is pointless since you've already blown it? Perhaps in your own case, you somehow believe in the necessity of faith but you say "It's very insignificant as long as I have the will to make my dreams fly?"

Well, back to the story for a moment. Jesus in verse twenty-three made yet another telling statement in response to the father's desperate plea. The sick boy's father said, *"If thou canst do anything, have compassion on us and help us."* Jesus said unto him, *"If thou canst believe,*

ALL THINGS (emphasis mine) are possible to him that believeth." This is truly liberating. By this Jesus revealed to the father his part in the possibility equation – faith.

Right there on the ground was his possessed child who wallowed foaming and right before him [the father] was the only condition to be satisfied for the fulfillment of the miracle he long sought for. 'If thou canst believe, all things are possible to him that believeth.'

Your dream, expected miracle, anticipated answer, or desired possibility is only your faith away. Everything you have ever wished for can be a reality right before your face just like it happened to the demon-possessed boy in our text when *"Jesus took him by the hand and lifted him up; and he arose"* (verse 27).

DO YOU BELIEVE?

The tapestry of life's fabric is woven with the fiber of challenges that constantly push the boundaries of our belief system. Circumstances will drive you to the point where you will be faced with the question of faith— "Do I believe?" Truth is, ready or not, life will beckon you to battle. But how will you fight? The bible tells us in 1John 5:4, *…and this is the victory that overcometh the world [everything that represents impossibility], even our faith.* Faith is pivotal to what you get out of life.

Faith is a choice. You either decide to fight that sickness, financial lack, family challenge or broken dream with your strength and wisdom or the other way round – weaponizing your faith!

Faith is resignation to God because you esteem Him faithful and able to carry you through whatever you might be going through and in whichever way He sees fit. Faith makes you laugh at impossibilities; it steadies your frame of mind and keeps you unruffled amidst troublous circumstances. It is the substance of things hoped for, the evidence of things not seen as the writer of the book of Hebrews puts it.

THE POSSIBILITIES OF THE POSSIBILITY FAITH

It Stills Your Soul

The immediate consequence of the possibility faith is rest. The rest of faith. It is your faith *"that maketh the storm a calm, so that the waves thereof are still"* (Psalm 107:29).

Thinking a vacation would do his family some good, Horatio Spafford sent his wife and four daughters on a ship to England, planning to join them after he finished some pressing business at home. However, while crossing the Atlantic Ocean, the ship was involved in a terrible collision and sunk. More than 200 people lost their lives, including all four of Horatio Spafford's precious daughters. His wife, Anna, survived the tragedy. Upon arriving in England, she sent a telegram to her husband that began: "Saved alone. What shall I do?"

Horatio immediately set sail for England. At one point during his voyage, the captain of the ship, aware of the tragedy that had struck the Spafford family, summoned Horatio to tell him that they were now passing over the spot where the shipwreck had occurred.

As Horatio thought about his daughters, words of comfort and hope filled his heart and mind. He wrote them down, and they have since become a well-beloved hymn:

> When peace like a river, attendeth my way,
>
> When sorrows like sea billows roll—
>
> Whatever my lot, thou hast taught me to know
>
> It is well, it is well with my soul.

It Banks On God's Unending Resources

Remember that earlier in this chapter we discussed that God runs an economy of 'all things.' Interestingly, your faith is the recognized currency for transactions in this economy. It has the capacity to place demands on the resources you need for the actualization of any dream you mind can conceive.

It Strengthens You Against All Odds

In his epistle to the Philippians, the Apostle Paul wrote, "*I can do ALL THINGS through Christ which strengthens me."* (Philippians 4:13). Faith in God, while we wait for His promise, gives an impartation of strength from Christ himself, enabling you to effortlessly climb every mountain before you. It is very indispensable. This strength is predicated on God's ability in and through you. If your heart will not fail or cringe beneath the weight of expectation, then the possibility faith must be your constant companion. Of this, David said in Psalms 73:26, *"...God is the strength of my heart and my portion forever."*

The story is told of Anne Johnson Flint, who by the age of 6 had lost both her parents. By the time she was in her teens, she had developed arthritis and soon after lost the use of her legs. Bedridden, she was covered with sores and lost control of her hands and many of her bodily functions.

If anyone could have been excused for writing dark and depressing lyrics it would have been a woman like Anne Flint. Instead, she focused on Jesus and the lyrics that she was inspired to write were of hope and faith.

"He Giveth More Grace"

He giveth more grace as the burdens grow greater,
He sendeth more strength as the labors increase,
To added afflictions He addeth His mercy,
To multiplied trials His multiplied peace.

His Love has no limit; His grace has no measure. His pow'r has no boundary known unto men. For out of His infinite riches in Jesus, He giveth, and giveth, and giveth again!

When we have exhausted our store of endurance,
When our strength has failed ere the day is half done,
When we reach the end of our hoarded resources,
Our Father's full giving is only begun.

It Purifies Your Character

On the other side of unshakeable faith in God during tough times is a refined and tempered character, a setting of the soul's gaze upon God and an aligning of the heart to suit the will and purposes of God. Think of Job, Abraham, Hannah, and Paul. What usually comes to mind is the beauty of a tried life sponsored by faith in God; the fineness of tempered mortar and purified gold – Precious!

In Job 13:15, Job spoke these very profound words, most probably in pain: *"Though He slay me, yet will I trust in Him: but I will maintain mine own ways before Him."*

And How Shall They Believe?

Romans 10:14 renders the full citation of the phrase above. It says, *how shall they call on him I whom they have not believed? And how shall they believe in him of whom they have not heard? And how shall they hear without a preacher?*

> Is the possibility faith an illusion? A mental, religious ideology to cajole the simple-minded?

"No."

So, can it be a personal possession?

"Yes."

But how is it obtained and sustained?

"The word of God"

That sounds like a dialogue right? Yes, a dialogue between you and I. The scriptures says in verse 17 of the same chapter of Romans, *So then, faith cometh by hearing and hearing by the word of God.*

Are you helplessly faithless? Then turn to the word of God. Is your faith weak and almost dead? Fix your gaze on the life-giving word with all your heart. Meditate on God (His magnificence) and God's promises (His benevolence) and you will fan to flame the fire of faith for all possibilities, for with God all things are possible!

3

YOU ARE NOT THE ONLY ONE

"Show me someone who has done something worthwhile, and I'll show you someone who has overcome adversity."

– **Lou Holtz**

Everyone experiences difficulties and challenges, and there can be no doubt about that. The fact that you're a possibility thinker or that you believe that anything is possible doesn't mean you won't come face to face with some challenges as you go through life. Nobody anticipates problems excitedly. I mean, have you ever met anyone who joyfully looks forward to challenges like a birthday surprise? I have never seen one and I don't think you will ever see one either. Why is this so? It's human nature to desire bliss with no pains, joys with no tears, and roses with no thorns. We fear challenges, pray so hard against them, and deeply wish heaven will be replicated now. Even though none of us looks forward to troubles or challenges, the Scripture declares that *"In this world, you will have tribulations"* (John 16:33). This passage posits clearly that having tribulations is not something any human being (rich, poor, young, old, black, white) can escape.

Whenever a new gadget is bought, the proper thing to do is to search the manual for specific instructions. I sometimes wish I could see all of my life spread out before me like a picture story. Maybe, if I saw the point where challenges would surface, I would cleverly avoid them or never put myself in situations that would warrant such challenges. Funny, isn't it? If wishes were horses, I would be riding so high by now. Life, however, is a mixture of highs and lows, curves and bends, cries, and laughter.

As long as we have breath, we are bound to encounter challenges on life's road. If I had the opportunity to choose how life would play out for me, I would choose a road with no bumps, a road where there are no obstacles to achieving my dreams. The truth that many people shy away from, however, is that challenges are common to humans, and as long as we are on planet earth, we would always be fighting the good fight of faith—the fight to accomplish our dreams. Yes, no one loves trouble; we all crave for a smooth journey. However, life is not designed to work that way.

Challenges are Universal

Life throws some bombshells at us when we least expect it. It sometimes leaves us sad, stuck, angry, or perplexed. However, it is in these challenges that the best of us is discovered; it is in challenges that the best inventions are created; challenges set our creative minds to work. It is in challenges that our eyes are open to better opportunities. I know you do not like being ruffled, but I want you to know today that being ruffled is something that is common to man and you are not the only one.

Let me briefly share with you a story from Andres Lara's *'Inspire the Sleeping Giant Within.*" It is a story that illustrates the fact that everyone faces challenges and that there are vital lessons or benefits we can get from every challenge that comes our way, depending on our attitude to it. It is a story that will inspire you to rise above the storms and see the beauty in your storm. According to the author, a woman, whose only son had died, went to see a prophet to ask for a potion that would help to free her life of pains.

"Fetch me a mustard seed from a home that has never known sorrow. We will use it to drive sorrow from your life" [said the prophet]. The woman went off at once in search of that magical seed.

She came first to a mansion and said to the owners, "I am looking for a home that has never known sorrow. Is this such a place?" They told her, "You've certainly come to the wrong place," and began to describe all the tragic things that recently had befallen them. The woman said to herself, "Who is better able to help these unfortunate people than I, who have had a misfortune of my own?"

She comforted them for a while, then went one with her search. But wherever she turned, she found one tale after another of sadness and misfortune. She became so involved in ministering to other people's grief that she ultimately forgot about her quest for the magical seed, never realizing that it had, in fact, driven the sorrow out of her life.

When I read this story, I could relate to every bit of it. It's pretty easy to go out on your porch and watch your neighbor, and wish you could swap lives and live his for the rest of your life. Your friend has a luxurious house, posh car, stunning wife, and a fantastic job. In your mind, you assume that everything is perfect for him. If only you could go more intimate with him and ask him serious questions about life, he'll tell you he's had his fair share of troubles.

If the first part of John 16:33 that I quoted earlier that says, *"In this world you will have tribulations"*, was all that God had to say to humanity, we would all have been hopeless. But thanks be God because the concluding part says, *"Be of good cheer, I have overcome the world."* This concluding part of that verse contains so much hope that can last you through whatever challenge you'd ever experience. Having a challenge is not a death sentence. If we approach or look at challenges with an eye of faith and a lens of positivity, we will have the capacity to turn those obstacles to opportunities.

I urge you, friend, to think less of your challenges and, instead, look forward to the miracles that will emerge from the many obstacles you have to contend with. Know also that several people have grappled with similar challenges and even greater and have come out shinning brighter and sharing wonderful testimonies. Believe it; it will soon be your turn if you can learn from their examples. Be assured that no problem can limit you; no thorn can stop your bloom, and no rain can stop the sunshine of the future.

Inspiring Examples

Joseph

Joseph is a famous character in the Bible that I never get tired of reading about. I know you would have read his story a good number of times and you may not be as interested in his story as you should be right now. Perhaps, Biblical stories do not speak to our hearts because we remove ourselves from such situations in our mental space and we also tend to forget that some of these stories were true-life occurrences. Now, let's get to the Biblical Joseph's story together. This time around, I want you to read with all your sensory organs in active mode.

Joseph was a young lad of seventeen with big dreams given to him from God. He was a pious, honest, and faithful young boy among 10 mischievous brothers, who hated him for his dreams and his insistence on living a righteous lifestyle. The Bible even records that he reported his brothers' evil actions to their father.

His father loved him specially because he was a son born in his old age and the son of his cherished wife, Rachel, whom he adored and served for 14 years before she became his wife. His father could not hide the special love he had for Joseph. He even sewed a special coat of many colors for him, and this made his brothers more jealous of him.

Innocent teenage Joseph kept narrating his dreams to his envious brothers and they hated him more. God gave him a dream and he told this dream to everybody- his father and brethren. He made so much noise about it and the hatred of his brothers grew the more. One day, his father told him to go to Shechem to check the welfare of his brothers in the field with the flocks and he gladly obeyed. It was that trip he made in love that led to him being sold into slavery.

This is Joseph, whom God gave the dream of a beautiful future. One would have taught that everything was going to run smoothly for him because of God's plan. But it didn't. Isn't it so sad to be sold to strangers like a piece of bread by brothers you call your own? Can you try to imagine the thoughts that would have run through his mind when his brothers sold him off to merchants? No doubt, he would have felt abandoned, hopeless, and frustrated. In fact, were it not for the intervention of Reuben, who counseled the other brothers not to shed blood, they were even ready to kill Joseph. How would you have felt if you brought food from a far place to your siblings and all they could do was strip you naked, throw you into a pit while they devoured the delicious meal you brought? How would you relate with God's precious promises of elevation and promotion, if you don't go down into the pit of demotion?

The merchants took him to Egypt and sold him to Potiphar, an officer of Pharaoh who was also the captain of the guard. Amid these challenges, God's hands never left him: *"And the LORD was with Joseph, and he was a prosperous man; and he was in the house of his master the Egyptian"* (Genesis 39:2). Even when he was thrown into prison on false allegations, God was still with him and favored him. This would be our experience too, irrespective of what challenges we face. As long as we trust God and believe firmly in Him, He will deliver us from every trouble. He did not promise us a life without fires and rivers; He only promised to be with us in the midst of all the storms and challenges.

The storms we encounter do not stop God from fulfilling His great promises concerning us. The storms only reinforce His greatness, and His sovereignty to use the foolish things of the world to confound the wise. Miracles have their sources in challenges; there won't be a need for miracles if there were no situations that tried and tested us.

One thing I love about Joseph was that he never allowed bitterness to take root in his heart. In every situation and circumstance, he offered the best of his service. He was faithful in honoring God in the face of temptations. Being the head servant to a captain of Pharaoh must have been a well-paying job for a migrant slave like him. It must have been a great temptation to concede to the carnal demands of Potiphar's wife. But he didn't. He would rather honor God and go to prison.

Some questions many have often asked are, where was God when his brothers sold him? Where was God when Potiphar's wife lied against him? Where was God when Potiphar did not bother to hear his side of the story? Where was God when Potiphar threw him into prison? All these are valid questions and I may not have all the answers. But one thing I believe and know is that God was right there in the midst of those challenges, channeling everything to culminate into the perfect future He promised Joseph.

Joseph kept touching lives with his talent even in prison. Though he suffered as an innocent man, he didn't mourn his predicament in self-pity but allowed his light to shine to others. He interpreted dreams to a fellow inmate who was a staff of Pharaoh. It was that act of kindness in the prison that led to his promotion as the second-in-command to the king in a strange land.

Through him, God rescued his entire family and kindred from famine. Through divine providence, his dreams came true eventually and his brethren paid homage to him after God exalted him.

Kris Carr

On Feb 14, 2003, Kris went for a regular check-up at the hospital and received the news that dramatically changed her life. She did not check-in at the hospital because she was sick or had some funny symptoms. She felt really good with herself and walked in happily to do a random health check. Walking out of the hospital, she became fully aware that she had a stage 4 incurable cancer called epithelioid hemangioendothelioma in her lungs and liver. She was 32 when she got the diagnosis and was given a time lag of 10 years before her death.

Now, this is the interesting part, instead of succumbing to the disease, Kris decided to challenge her diagnosis head-on by initiating new plant-based nutritional lifestyles. She became an inspiration to thousands of people through her experiences. Her website has over 40,000 subscribers. This transformation did not happen overnight. Like anyone diagnosed with a terminal disease, her world came crashing down initially and it was as if her life shattered into irredeemable pieces. However, she was able to rise above the obscure situation she found herself in by shinning her light.

Her experience and journey have brought much hope

to thousands of people in the world. Through her pain, she became a beacon of hope to many. She realized she never truly lived before cancer. Cancer was meant to break her, but she allowed the challenge to give her a brand-new perspective about life. Let's review some of her words together:

"As I meditate on the impact that illness has had on my life, I realize I'm a better, more grateful woman today because of cancer. I was asleep at the wheel before cancer shook me awake. And though there's still no cure, I continue to live harmoniously with cancer".

A lot of people are like the old Kris. They are usually like the baby eagle who wants to stay all day in the nest. The mother eagle, however, knows that her eaglet cannot survive the assignment of the future if it does not leave the comfort zone. It is in leaving the comfort zone that skill, expertise, character, and experience are formed. So, what does the mother eagle do? The mother eagle shakes the nests vigorously and even upturns it. This way, the baby eagle is left with no option than to fly. It is in the problem or challenge instigated by the mother eagle that the eaglet grows into maturity.

Kris Carr was just taking life easy; she was not influencing anyone positively and no one was influencing her positively too. Cancer jolted her from her long 32-year sleep and made her realize that life was truly short, and that the essence of true living was in touching lives, being truly happy, and being intentional about daily living and choices. It's over 10 years now and she's lived passed her predicted death day. She is living a productive and fulfilling life because she intentionally looked beyond her sickness and found many more reasons to be happy and grateful.

Speaking about her present condition and how she feels, this is what she said: *"I've been living with cancer for over a decade and it has taught me so much about taking care about myself and living my life to the fullest. This jolting moment sparked a deep desire in me to stop holding back and start participating in my wellbeing. Though I can't be cured, I can still be healthy. I can still feel better, love harder and have a more joyful life. So, I hit the road on a self-care pilgrimage and haven't looked back. More than a decade later, my life is more magical than it was before my diagnosis".*

Today, she has become a New York Times bestseller, author of five best-selling books, a wellness coach, with an award-winning documentary film about her life.

Galaxy of Exemplars

There are so many other inspiring stories of great people who surmounted one obstacle or another before they reached their zenith. Actually, there's nothing incredible, laudable, or impactful in our world that didn't come with a price. Can we ever talk about Abraham Lincoln, Nelson Mandela, Oral Roberts, Ibukun Awosika, Nick Vujicic, Strive Masiyiwa, Mike Bamiloye, Corrie Ten Boom, Mary Slessor and a host of successful men and women without talking about the many mountains they had to climb before getting astounding results?

What then did these people do differently? How were they able to come out stronger and better despite the problems they contended with? How were they able to maintain their focus and keep on striving until they succeeded? What lessons can you learn from them on how should you handle your challenges? Do you just do nothing and allow the problems to swallow you? Should you run away and hide? I'll talk about these in later chapters.

As we gradually draw the curtain for this amazing introductory chapter, I want to remind you again that you are not the only one experiencing a difficult situation in your life. Challenges are a part of life and we need to learn to make them stepping stones to greater heights. I want you to know that there is nothing you are facing that cannot turn out to be a blessing. If other people can use their attitude and perspective to convert distracting situations to their advantage, you also can do it. Yes, you can!

So, arise and shine! Wipe the tears from your eyes. Wear a smile. Leap for joy. Rejoice, for you know that the Lord is your strength and song. He will not leave you hopeless and He is right there with you working out His best for your life. I know that it is sometimes hard to believe God's truth about you when it doesn't make any sense. Maybe you have cried, prayed and fasted for many days and your reality negated your expectation. Do not lose hope. Resist the urge to utter negative words in such situations. Be still and find solace in the Word of God. Read inspiring stories of people who have faced similar challenges and have overcome them. Be still and know that everything good can still flow from God's cistern of love to you, regardless of the storm.

4

PRINCIPLES OF POSSIBILITY THINKING

"Many little steps, joined one after the other, is what makes success possible. Keep doing little stuffs every day. Don't give up!"

– **Israelmore Ayivor**

What set winners apart is not necessarily their natural talents and abilities, appearances, or connections, it is the mentality they bring to every situation. This mentality is characterized and driven by some core principles, which we shall be unravelling and examining here. Mentality, by the way, means a characteristic way of thinking or an established frame of mind.

Now, I believe that with all we have seen in the previous chapters you should have realized that you are a potential champion! Yes, your reality may say contrary but that's because you are yet to tweak your mind into a winning mode. You can and you should do great things because you have what it takes right there within you. And to do great things, you need a mental paradigm shift, the strategies for which we about to explore.

ANATOMY OF A WINNER'S MIND

It's been proven that what sets champions apart is neither the connections they have, their appearances nor even their natural abilities; but the mindset they bring into the game. You need to develop a certain type of mindset; the kind that champions possess: one that leaves no chance for negativity. What does this kind of mind look like? Let's take a peek into the mind of a typical champion to see the principles that govern their mindset.

1. Champions have a strong faith in God and themselves. All true champions in life have a relationship with God. This relationship and reliance on God naturally boost confidence that makes them approach any problem with a strong conviction that they will overcome. The story of young David readily comes to mind here. Ordinarily, David had no business confronting Goliath on the battlefield. Judging from their resume, taking on Goliath was a suicide mission, but David had a strong faith in God that gave him the confidence to look a giant in the eye and say: *"This day will the LORD deliver thee into mine hand; and I will smite thee,* *and take thine head from thee; and I will give the carcases of the host of the Philistines this day unto the fowls of the air, and to the wild beasts of the earth*" (1Samuel 17: 46). The mind of the champion brims with confidence in a higher power—God-- and in themselves.

2. Champions have a growth mindset. They understand that they need to constantly improve themselves so they are always enthusiastic about learning new things, no matter the height they have attained. They are always on the lookout for opportunities or information that will help them to continuously improve their craft. People with a growth mindset don't just rely on innate gifts and abilities, they believe that continuous learning, coupled with hard-work, network, and a good strategy will help them get to the top of the ladder.

3. Champions are mentally tough and resilient. This attribute comes from an understanding that attaining anything worthwhile will be attended by different kinds of challenges and obstacles. So, the champion resolves not to cower in the face of challenges but to think of a way around the problem. This kind of mindset is not deterred by setbacks, negative public opinions, limitations, or whatever other kinds of hindrance. Rather, it feels excited to tackle the challenges. Again, I must remind you that this kind of resilience has roots in the strong belief in God and self.

4. Champions take charge of their minds. If you were asked the question "who is in charge of your mind?" how would you respond? Champions understand the importance of having a presence of mind-mindfulness. They don't allow their minds to roam about; they intentionally focus their thoughts on events, memories, or plans that will bring about progress. They are constantly dragging their minds off any form of negativity. This, they practice until they gain a mastery of their minds. They control and decide what the mind dwells on so that the mind doesn't get fixated on any form of negativity.

5. Champions don't quit. I will spend a little more on this in the next chapter, but let me say here that life is never a smooth sail; sometimes you are given a cause to laugh or cry. Sometimes you soar like the eagle and other times you fall flat on your face. It happens to everyone, but champions are what they are because they won't sit back, throw up their hands, and give up. They look back at the situation leading to their fall, learn the lessons, get up, and move on. They don't allow themselves to get stuck by what life throws at them. No! They make the most of it because they are committed to success.

6. Champions have a strong support system. They understand that to achieve greatness, you must surround himself with people who love you and want to see you succeed. These people could come in form of mentors, friends, family members, and acquaintances who understand your dreams and can make meaningfully contributions. They don't isolate themselves and think they have it all figured. They humble themselves to learn from and network with others.

7. Champions are broadminded. Narrow-minded people will always limit themselves; this is why you cannot afford to be narrow-minded. Champions are willing to consider other people's opinions and suggestions. Unlike narrow-minded people, they are free from prejudice or bias. This does not stop them from being assertive about their own opinions and beliefs, but they would always consider all the options before making a decision.

STEPS TO POSSIBILITY THINKING

This process begins with a choice: a decision to be the main player in your own success story. When it dawns on you that your success is your responsibility; one that is intrinsically linked to your mindset, then you are on your way to changing any undesirable situation around you. To develop a Champion's mentality, you need to reprogram your mind: you need to do something like a resetting of your mind. Confront your belief system, sift through it and discard the ones that have been counter-productive thus far. Then, deliberately choose to believe things that agree with your dream or desired goals. Reprograming your mind and developing a champion's mindset is not as easy as it sounds, but you can achieve it easily if you conscientiously work at it. To get this done, you need to practice the following.

1. Visualize what you want. Have a mental picture of what you really want. Make sure it is a specific desire because the mind does respond to vague, ambiguous desires. Put yourself in the exact situation you will rather be. Savor it and see it happening.

2. Practice written affirmation. Put down your desires and goals in black and white. Writing down your goals will give you a visual reminder of where you are going and what you need to do to get there. It's been recommended that you write it as many times as 20-25 times each day for a month because what you focus on has a way of expanding itself. This may seem unconventional and out of the box, but as you write down your goals every day, the message begins to take root in your subconscious mind, solidifying your vision internally.

3. Engage in oral affirmation. This involves making a positive declaration about your goals. It is more like self-prophesying. Engaging in repetitive positive affirmation can change the neural pathway in the brain, said Dr. Mona L. Schulz, a neuropsychiatrist. When this happens, you find that you are spurred towards taking actions based on your new belief. For example when you say to yourself *"I will do my best to be the best."* You will find your actions tilting towards doing your best at what you do. We'll delve more into the power of positive confessions in chapter 7.

4. Meditation. This involves a great deal of mindfulness; that is, training the mind to focus on a thought, an object or activity to get clarity and calmness. Meditation makes the mind more responsive to whatever thought/ or belief you want to establish in the mind. Apart from helping you to be focus and calm, meditation also helps you to be more rational, less anxious and stressed; you become more creative, and your memory improves dramatically.

5. Positive self-talk. This is different from making declarative statements about yourself or your situation. It involves having a positive conversation with yourself. Why is this important? The truth is you will most likely believe what you say to yourself, and this will affect your mood, responses, decisions, and attitude. You should never be caught saying negative things to yourself, no matter the situation. The Bible says that **"David encouraged himself in the LORD his God"** (1 Samuel 30:6). At this point in his life, he and his men had lost everything they had: their families and their possessions. David's men were so distraught that they blamed David and even thought of stoning him out of frustration. Imagine that kind of situation. At this crucial time, it would have taken a great deal of effort not to remain despondent, but David must have reminded himself that there was a God who specializes in doing the impossible, therefore, all hope was not lost. He must have cheered himself up with this fact, prompting him to enquire from God, what his next step should be. Again, be your own cheerleader and motivator; don't rely on others. Make it a point of duty to say positive things to yourself at all times and you will be amazed at the result. I'll talk more about the power of positive confessions in the next chapter.

6. Act out your dream. As you work on reprograming your mind, you need to begin to conduct yourself as if your dreams were already fulfilled. You want to be a champion? Find out how champions behave and begin to act and talk like them. As you make an effort to visualize your desired situation and you act as if you have already achieved this, you are technically tuning the mind to this reality.

7. Learn something every day. This is one of the best ways to program your mind for success. A champion is willing and open to learning so they can increase in knowledge and get to know how to chart the course outside their comfort zone. Read something every day; learn something new from time to time. Talk and listen to know legible people: there are free Podcasts available online; attend seminars and workshops, constantly put yourself in a position where you can learn. Charlie Tremendous Jones once said *"you will be the same person in five years as you are today except for the people you meet and the books you read."*

If you are going to be a winner in life, you need to make that choice, visualize it, show up, take action, persist and you will be singing a victory song.

Guard Your Imaginations

Someone has rightly said that "the mind can be the harshest battleground. It can be the place where the greatest conflicts are carried out." You will always be confronted with all kinds of thoughts. You will be made to choose between negative and positive thoughts. Your choice will influence your behavior and responses to life.

In *Battlefield of the Mind*, Joyce Meyer said something that spoke to me and I will like to share it here. She said, *"The Bible says that a tree is known by its fruit. The same is true in our lives. Thoughts bear fruit. Think good thoughts, and the fruit in your life will be good. Think bad thoughts, and the fruit in your life will be bad. You can actually look at a person's attitude and know what kind of thinking is prevalent in his life. A sweet, kind person does not have mean, vindictive thoughts. By the same token, a truly evil person does not have good, loving thoughts. Remember Proverbs 23:7 and allow it to have an impact on your life: for as you think in your heart, so are you."*

If you see anyone who says it's impossible to achieve something, do know that the defeat started from the mind. If the mind accepts defeat, then there is nothing more to it. The bible says, out of the abundance of the heart, the mouth speaks. Also, the thing that defiles a man is not from the outside, rather, it is from the inside. If the devil can defeat your mind through negative thoughts, then he has defeated you already. Guide your thoughts. If you don't, the devil will litter all manner of rubbish there. But you can decide what kind of thought to give attention to. The bible says in the book of Philippians 4:8 (KJV), *"Finally, brethren, whatsoever things are true, whatsoever things are honest, whatsoever things are just, whatsoever things are pure, whatsoever things are lovely, whatsoever things are of good report; if there be any virtue, and if there be any praise, think on these things."*

Do not allow negativity to becloud your thoughts and reasoning. Defeat starts from your thoughts; the same way victory starts from the thoughts. Train your mind to think about positive things. The same way you speak God's Word is the same way you should think God's Word. But you can't think the Word if it's not in you. This is to say your greatest weapon in defeating negative thoughts is the Word of God. The Word of God boosts your faith. Faith comes by hearing, and hearing the Word of God! Even Jesus used the weapon of the Word in the wilderness to defeat the devil. (Luke 4:1-13.) Each time the devil lied to Him, Jesus responded with, "It is written," and quoted him the Word."

As you take the steps listed above to develop your mind, you must have a strong grip on your thought life too; take charge of it. Taking responsibility for your thought is to notice what goes on in your mind and make a conscious effort to put your thought under control. You can't claim ignorance for what happens in your mind or claim the devil, circumstances or people are responsible for what goes on in your mind. God holds you responsible for your thoughts, for "... *[He] is a discerner of the thoughts and intents of the heart. Neither is there any creature that is not manifest in his sight: but all things are naked and opened unto the eyes of him with whom we have to do.*" so you can't afford to be passive about your mind. Someone said, "*Whatever your innermost dominant thought is focused on is what you attract, move towards, or become."* This, of course, implies that you can't be passive about the activities in your mind, and allow negative thoughts to take over your mind. You must conscientiously take responsibility for your thought life.

Age or stature is not the major determinant of what you can achieve but the kind of mindset you have. Take David for example, he was only a youth who was expected to run errands; but because he had a mindset that only thought in tandem with God's power, he only did challenged Goliath, he defeated him. When you think in line with God's power, you can face challenges that would have ordinarily scare you. Like David, you might be facing challenges that other experienced people like Saul will avoid. Let this register in your mind that the fight is the Lord's and not yours.

David was just a youth but he was conscious of the fact that he carried in him a personality stronger than the giant, Goliath. Knowing the power of God, he didn't entertain discouragement despite dissuasion from his brother and even Saul. Although Goliath disdained David, he didn't mind, because David knew whom he trusted. You could imagine what David was thinking when he proceeded to challenge the experienced warrior. He didn't see Goliath's stature that scared experienced adults but he rather saw the might of God in his mind's eyes. He must have thought of God as being mightier than Goliath. He must have thought of how God helped him kill the lion and the bear as his testimony before

Saul revealed (Samuel 17:36). He couldn't have trusted in the sling and the stones. He who thinks in line with God's power sees as God sees and is not intimidated. Such a person doesn't belittle himself because he knows the authority backing him up. He trusted in the God of Israel for whom he was zealous. That was what gave David the confidence and courage to swing into action.

Just like David, a victor in thought and action does not fear or avoid challenges. You don't fear persecution or opposition. You don't succumb to dissuasion from men. You can see your triumph over seemingly unconquerable obstacles of life through the power of God in your mind's eyes. Simply think, talk, and act in faith like David. You can do the ordinary (like David's sling and stones) to achieve the extraordinary. How did David defeat Goliath? He thought about his previous victory; he saw the present victory in his mind's eyes; he confessed it and acted on it. You must also do likewise. There are occasions you don't keep quiet. It will take you speaking back at the enemy at times. Don't sit back in self-pity. Challenge the enemy (the unwanted circumstances) as David did. Seek victory, see it, say it, and share it. Stop worrying about it. Share testimonies that will further strengthen your courage. Whereas David used physical stones, our stone is the Word of God; *"For the word of God is quick, and powerful, and sharper than any two edged sword, piercing even to the dividing asunder of soul and spirit..."* (Hebrew 4; 12). The Word of God is still as effective as ever, capable of overcoming every obstacle. Remember Jesus Himself overcame temptations with the Word of God in the wilderness. So confess the word of God into that situation and you will definitely have testimonies to share.

Belief and Unbelief

Belief and unbelief are two factors or forces that we must quickly consider here. Belief is an aspect of a positive mental attitude. Wikipedia defines belief as a *"state of* mind *in which a person thinks something to be the case, with or without there being empirical evidence to prove that something is the case with factual certainty."* Do you believe great possibilities? Do you believe in your dream? Do you believe in God? *"Today, some Christians are content to merely exist until they die. They don't want to risk anything, to believe God, to grow or mature. They refuse to believe his Word, and have become hardened in their unbelief. Now they're living just to die"* (David Wilkerson).

Like the concave lens used in focusing solar energy on earthly objects, belief is the force that focuses on the power of your mind to achieve your aspirations in life. Your mind has the potentials but belief is that force that gathers and concentrates your thoughts on your desires with irresistible intensity for optimum achievement. Strong belief does not entertain any iota of doubt because it has burnt the bridge behind it—no going back. It penetrates every impediment. When you attain this level of belief, you will be consumed with the desire for what you need to achieve. It creates a mental picture of your desires such that they appear to be physically visible.

You can make your dream a reality by believing that you can. Jesus, the author of life confirms this reality when He says, *"If ye have faith as a grain of mustard seed, ye shall say unto this mountain, Remove hence to yonder place; and it shall remove; and nothing shall be impossible unto you"* (Matthew17:20). Faith is synonymous with belief. And it is apparent from Jesus' assertion that there is no obstacle you cannot overcome if you believe. Mountains are no threats to them that believe. What is it that is threatening you from taking the next step in achieving your dream? Choose to believe God today and success will be yours!

You must, however, do away with fear and doubt if you will be successful in life. Fear and doubt are two related elements that hamper progressive thoughts. Fear is poisonous to any ambitious mind. It fosters doubt. And, unfortunately, some people have fixed their minds on fear of failure. What if I try this and fail? What if I take this step and fail to succeed? Their minds are filled with "what ifs". They fail to realize that fear and doubt weaken the force of the mind in achieving its desires. Instead of picturing your goal, it is fear and doubts you have magnified and made so real in your mind's eyes. Hasn't your mind been chained with fear and doubt already? Break yourself loose from the powers of fear and doubt and let the power of your mind be released to think progressively. Even the Bible says that fear has torment (John 4:18). The torment of fear is so severe that it almost deactivates your mind as soon as it surfaces. It is pitiable that many people who should have set international records in their respective endeavors are limited by these monsters called fear and doubt.

Have you ever had an experience where fear kills your joy and enthusiasm over a particular goal you intended to achieve? Yes! That is how fear operates. It is a dream killer. It kills every element of courage you have to pursue a goal. It makes you disbelieve yourself. And tell me, how can you realize your dream without believing in yourself and God's promises? Fear makes you believe you cannot meet up with whatever standards that have been set. And this is capable of leaving you completely demoralized if you don't discard such thoughts. Consequently, you must believe in yourself if you must achieve your dream. Are you already putting off that project because you feel it's an impossible task? Don't give up yet. You can accomplish it. Dale Carnegie encourages: "Do the thing you fear to do and keep on doing it…that is the quickest and surest way ever yet discovered to conquer fear."

You can attain any height in your endeavor if you can maximally utilize your thought pattern. You must not be limited by a negative mindset. You have potentials that must be harnessed to achieve your dreams. It is, however, important to know that what you think, believe, and confess as your need and aspiration can only be granted according to God's will. That is why it was being emphasized earlier that your thoughts must align with God's will, but shouldn't be limited by human factors. *"God shall supply all your need according to his riches in glory by Christ Jesus"* (Philippians 4:19) as you consider all that has been said in this chapter, you too will be celebrated as the next champion in Jesus Name.

5

THE POWER OF YOUR WORDS

"Words are containers for power, you choose what kind of power they carry." - **Joyce Meyer**

No doubt, what you say is a direct manifestation of your thought. For out of the abundance of the heart, the mouth speaks (Matthew 12:34). And just so you know, there is a great deal of power in your tongue. There is a mystery behind spoken words that can ultimately help improve your life. The first and most compelling proof of this is that everything around you came into existence because words were spoken. This implies that your words, to a large extent, have some influence over your life. These thoughts are manifested when you lend them a voice. And they subsequently become your experience.

The Bible says that the power of life and death is in the tongue

(Proverbs 18:21). This suggests that the force of the tongue can kill or give hope. So, beware of the words of your mouth. What kind of words escapes your lips? Are they words that give life or words that kill? You hear people uttering words like 'I don't know why I am so unfortunate? I don't think I will ever make it in this life. And a host of other words in that category. I tell you what, if you constantly speak and affirm negative words, they will come to be. Words are powerful, the more reason you should be deliberate about the words you utter.

Possibility Confessions

Possibility confessions suggest that you speak a desired condition into existence even though your present situation holds no evidence of the fulfillment of that desire. In the world today, more people, are embracing science, meaning that they live in/and embrace reality, which often leads to negative confessions. It is even more disheartening that Christians make up the lot of these Rationalists and while there are some things rational about Christianity, most of our peculiarities cannot be understood by the natural man (1 Corinthians 2: 14).

When hard times come, and we continue to confess the things we see: oh, things are hard, I can't make it, this man will defeat me, this school cannot admit me, hmmm, I'll assure you about one thing, it will be difficult to have it happen otherwise. When the devil brings up an issue in your life and you dwell so much on the things he's doing, without considering that there is A FATHER UP ABOVE who is willing to do greater things for you, the devil is happy because your confessions are proofs that you notice that he is there and that, my dear, is the aim of the devil. Why not confess the things that God has said concerning you? The scripture says that when they shall say there is a casting down, we will say there is a lifting up (Job 22:29). The promises in God's word are for all those that trust and love him. So, why do Christians forget these words when they are faced with hard times? We question God, murmur, and grumble, to the same God that has made things move well for them all the while. The Lord has done these things for us in the past and you think he cannot do more? He's not a God with a limit to what he can do.

As Christians, we should emulate the life of our father. He spoke the world into being. He said "let there be light" and there was. This means that even the father understands the efficacy of positive declaration which is why He commands in His word that we speak positive things. The father understands the results positive confessions can bring one's way. When we speak positive things, we call on our heavenly Father for a change in our situation and He, in turn, answers. In our case as Christians, we do not keep count of how many times we speak positively as the Bible says we always overcome by the words of our testimony. Words are powerful enough to make you a wonder or a wanderer on the earth. The saints of old, through the inspiration of the Holy Spirit, have versified in the Scripture the power of words.

In Proverbs 12 verse 18, the Scripture gives us a clear understanding of what words can do: *"There is that speaketh like the piercings of a sword; but the tongue of the wise is health."* This verse of scripture doesn't express the tongue as an organ in the body but as a producer of words. The words that proceed from the mouth of a wise man are health to him because he understands the benefits of making positive confessions. Health means he speaks good things into his life, irrespective of the uproar around him. Speaking like the piercings of a sword is not far from he that speaks negative words all the time. He considers all that is around him and makes confessions based on them.

When words are spoken, an atmosphere is let loose, either positive or negative, which depends on what was spoken and the belief system. You may ask yourself, how do these positive words proceed out of my mouth with all the negativity around? That's a question I will answer in this chapter. There is a link between what you hear, believe, and speak. The Scripture states faith cometh by hearing, and hearing what? The word of God. When you speak, you have to believe what you have said based on the undeniable truth of God's word. Stop feeding yourself with the negativity around you and start feeding off of what will build your faith and cause you to trust totally on him that has made all these promises in his word. The lord is ready to fulfill his promises and make your life all perfect again but you have to believe his promises.

Jesus Christ our Lord promised that we will command mountains to be removed and they will go (Matthew 21:21). One thing you need to understand is that the Lord Himself understood the power of spoken words and we are commanded in God's word to emulate this lifestyle. Jesus never shied from doing all he has commanded that we do. He once passed by a fig tree and saw that it was not yielding fruits. All He had to do was speak the word and the tree was gone. He was and is still the standard for His beloved children. Just confess positively to that situation and in no time, it shall become dim.

What causes all these changes? Just these four letters: WORD. Isn't it amazing that four letters can make you ten times better than you envisaged? You shall bind a thing on Earth and it shall be bound in heaven. When prayers are made, words proceed out of the mouth to the father. These words are powerful enough to cause a crumbling life to bubble again. The father says whatsoever you shall ask in prayer, believing, you shall receive. When you speak the words and believe them, your answer is ready. That's the arithmetic of receiving from God.

Confessing positively has a lot of benefits. Joel Osteen had come to the understanding of the extent words can go, which is why he opined that "you can change your world by changing your words". Words can create or destroy. I know no one, in his right mind, will want to destroy his life with his own hands, but many lives have been lost mainly due to reality-based confessions. If you want to put your life back together, start feeding on the word of God to renew your mind. Happiness in the face of challenges, motivation to do better, abundant blessings on Earth and in heaven, to mention but a few, are some of the blessings you enjoy for confessing positively. You may have been involved in the worst of all cases but what I tell you is real, begin to confess positively.

Optimism is the belief that only good things will happen. Being optimistic cannot be equated with telling a lie while positive confessions are a visible and hearable expression of that optimism. It is saying what your father has said concerning you. Being optimistic in all situations should be the behavior of a child of God because the Joy of the Lord is the strength of the believer. This means focusing the beam on Jesus always. Yes, this goes a long way in motivating someone to push forward in whatever he may be trying to achieve. It is knowing that no matter what I see or feel, the best is still before me.

Many people today emphasize the fact that one must be prepared for all possible outcomes of every situation including the worst. But I tell you today, prepare always for the best because your father has not told you the worst is going to come with it. Do not be caught in the web of those that are filled with so much negativity because they have a way of influencing you. Friendship is about influence. It's a two-way affair: you are getting influenced or you are the influencer. The group you belong to has a way of causing you to confess positively. When you are always in the midst of those that have negative belief systems, it's going to be difficult for you to have a positive belief system. Therefore, surround yourself with believers that are positive-minded.

Well, do you not think that your belief system needs a change? Have you ever wondered why you cannot do better when you say it? Have you ever wondered why people around you are doing so well and only you are relegated to the background? I tell you today that it has a lot to do with your belief system.

Granted that so many things around you can be very discouraging, but as a believer, do you succumb to the ill-health Satan has brought your way? The songwriter says "I'm not afraid of the darkness, whom shall I fear if God's before me, what shall we say to these things? I'm not afraid anymore". The reason the devil defeats most believers is because he has been able to instill fear in them, which clouds their understanding and recollection of the promises that God has made concerning their welfare.

I was told of the story of a man, who, at night, when he heard a frightening sound at his window, just laughed so hard and in no time, the sound was gone. If the devil is given a space in a believer's life, he wants to take over all which is always a bad end. The scripture says the Lord has raised a standard against the devil, to the point that he cannot succeed trying to bring you down. So when he comes to show his presence, you show him your essence which is God's existence. He cannot but flee because he fears a very confident and praying believer. The Scripture says the tongue is a little member but its capabilities are not restricted to or measured by its size. It looks somewhat insignificant because it's not one of the organs in the body that is conspicuous except the mouth is open.

Have you noticed that those organs we cannot see cause more chaos to the body than the conspicuous ones? Therefore, what comes out of your mouth has to have been carefully considered by you before it is let out. The scripture says that a man that calls himself a believer and does not bridle his tongue, his religion is vain. This further gives us a clearer picture of the words of a believer. The Father has said every word spoken will be accounted for. As believers, we have something different from what others possess and that is why we should not live like them but hold on to the one we have loved. Let your words be filled with grace and seasoned with salt as a believer. When the father says you should command that situation to go and you say otherwise, that's disobedience and you know the consequence of disobedience according to scriptures. So, why put yourself in a particular spot because of the words you speak? When things are not working out, they are because the same thing has been on the routine: a lot of negative confessions. A wise man once said to get a different result, try something new. Therefore, try to confess positively and you will see the change you have been expecting all this while coming to fruition.

Now let's talk about the relationship between the belief system and what is confessed. According to the *Oxford Advanced Learner's Dictionary*, belief is a strong feeling that somebody or someone exists and the confidence that something or someone is good or right. In the same vein, a confession is a statement that a person makes, admitting that they are guilty of a crime. Like has been mentioned earlier in this chapter, confession, in this present dispensation, tilts towards the negative aspect but speaking of positive confession, the tables are being turned around. When you believe that something is true, you find it much easier to let such out of your mouth because there is an assurance of its existence. Words are singularly the most powerful force available to humanity. It's what makes humans different from other species of living things on the planet. All the words that a person knows are stored in the lexicon.

The lexicon is the vocabulary of a person, language, or branch of knowledge. All the words that a person has acquired over time are stored there. These words are picked up from everything around a person. Faith comes by hearing and hearing the word of God. When one has been feeding off the word of God, making negative confessions is going to be far-fetched. Joshua chapter one verse eight paraphrased, says that the book of the law shall not depart from your mouth but you will meditate therein day and night, that you may observe to do according to all that is written therein; then you will make your way prosperous and have success. This was God's instruction to Joshua in Joshua 1:8. *"This book of the law shall not depart from your mouth"* means the things present in the scripture must be your daily confessions. When meditation on the word of God becomes consistent, deviation from its commands loses constancy.

The verse comes to a close with the phrase *"have good success"*. This means meditation, speaking, and doing the word equals success. Your negativity all this while has pushed you away from your desired destination. Most of us are fond of saying "no negative vibe, positive vibes only." Being around people that encourage you is better than the success itself because, in the long run, those positive words help make you better.

FIVE STEPS TO ENSURING POSSIBILITY CONFESSIONS

1. Draw closer to the Father that has promised you all these wonderful things in his word. He exalts his word more than his name, says the scriptures. When you talk to him about the hurt, he takes you away from that hurt of sorrow and brings you into a life that's sorted. He says in his word, that if you humble yourself and seek him, he will answer and cause healing on the bleeding hearts. Drawing closer is made easy when you know who you are getting

close to. If you have known the Father, draw closer and if not, you have to know him.

2. Feed on His Word because that ensures that you are in the right state of mind to confess positive things. Confess his word and see him ward off the plots of the devil with his flaming sword to bring you to the realization that He is ever-present as your Warlord. He will fight for you. Also, read books and Christian literatures that tell you more about the faithfulness of the father.

3. Hang around those with a positive mindset is a catalyst to the realization of your desired echelon. People who surround you, more often than not, influence you to be better or worse. Therefore, surround yourself with those that give positive vibes and will go to any Godly extent to see you get better.

4. Make a conscious effort to say positive things. You have to be intentional about it. You have to make the choice to speak these things or not. Remember, words are free but the way you use them may cost you. Confess positively and let go of the negativity.

5. Teach others about what has worked for you has a way of making that experience unforgettable. When your life is filled with positive confessions and you teach others to do so, it will stick perfectly to your heart and mind.

These steps will ensure that you are on the right track with your words. The promises of Christ are replete in the scriptures about, your progress, promotion, provision, prosperity, and protection.

PROGRESS

"Commit thy works unto the Lord, and thy thoughts shall be established" (Proverbs 16:3)

"The righteous also shall hold on his way, and he that hath clean hands shall be stronger and stronger" (Job 17:9).

PROMOTION

"For promotion cometh neither from the East, nor from the West, nor from the south. For God is the judge: he putteth down one, and setteth up another" (Psalms 75:6-7).

" Humble yourselves therefore under the mighty hand of God, that he may exalt you in due time" (1 Peter 5:6).

PROVISION

"O fear the lord, ye his saints: for there is no want to them that fear him" (Psalms 34:9).

"And God is able to make all grace abound toward you; that ye, always having all sufficiency in all things, may abound to every good work" (2 Corinthians 9:8).

PROSPERITY

"The liberal soul shall be made fat: and he that watereth shall be watered also himself" (Proverbs 11:25).

"The soul of the sluggard desireth, and hath nothing: but the soul of the diligent shall be made fat" (Proverbs 13:4).

PROTECTION

"The angel of the lord encampeth round about them that fear him, and delivereth them. O taste and see that the Lord is good: blessed is the man that trusteth in him" (Psalms 34:7-8).

"But the lord is faithful, who shall stablish you, and keep you from evil" (2 Thessalonians 3:3).

Therefore, forget the words from family and friends. They said it has always been this way, it cannot get better, your grandparents, parents, and siblings have passed through same and you have to also, no one has ever done it; I tell you, believe the word of God, as you speak it and you will scale through. The starting point of possession is confession. So, say it as many times as you can, LOUD AND CLEAR till it becomes as undeniable as $1+1=2$.

6

MAKE YOUR LIFE INTENTIONAL

"An unintentional life accepts everything and does nothing. An intentional life embraces only the things that will add to the mission of significance." **- John C. Maxwell**

Men and women who go on to achieve the seemingly impossible are ordinary people who take deliberate actions toward their desired haven. They don't just think their dreams are possible, they also make it possible.

You can never become what you've been destined to be or achieve your dreams if you don't make your life intentional. Life is full of distractions, some of which can even seem legitimate. Consequently, if you don't take steps towards living an intentional life, you will be caught doing unnecessary things that contribute nothing to your goals. At the end of the day, you discover that you have wasted your time, achieving nothing.

Living an intentional life is a principle you must adopt if you want to have good outcomes and get closer to fulfilling your purpose. You cannot afford to live by chance or by the "anything goes" slogan. No, you can't. one reason many possibility thinkers don't fulfil their dreams is because they don't take concrete and intentional steps to transform their dreams into reality.

How do you live an intentional life you may ask? I'll show you. But first of all, why do we need to live an intentional life?

- Intentional living helps you live life in an ordered manner. You don't do things for doing sake; rather, you realize that actions and decisions have consequences and therefore weigh the potential outcomes of the choices you make in life.

- Intentional living helps you detect and reject whatever could be injurious to your purpose and calling.

- Intentional living guides you to determine what you pay attention to, what you accept, the kind of places you go to, the kind of friends you keep, and the kind of activities or projects you embark on.

- Intentional living boosts your self-esteem and helps you exude confidence, knowing well that you are in control of you affairs.

- Intentional living will cause you to take responsibility for your actions. You live a life with minimal errors, maximum impact, zero excuse and absolutely no regrets!

PROCESS OF LIVING AN INTENTIONAL LIFE

Let's take a look at some of the steps you can take to help you live an intentional life every blessed day.

1. Pursue your passion

Living a life of possibilities requires that you have a cause to wake up each morning, eager to face the new day. When you're passionate about something, it will come with an inner drive that will serve as a propelling force to make you willingly invest your time, energy and resources into it. It becomes something you care for deeply, pursue with fervor and fight for with every ounce of you. Ever wondered why some famous people ended up committing suicide or dying of drug overdose even when it appeared they had the 'perfect' life? This foregrounds the truth that fame or wealth does not guarantee a sense of fulfillment; what gives true satisfaction is the accomplishment of your dreams and purpose in life.

2. Take responsibility for your life

A lot of times, we tend to blame people for the bad outcomes of our decisions. This happens when we hand over the power of taking decisions that affects our lives to others. It is your life. The earlier you wake up to the fact that you are responsible for whatever happens to you, the better for you. Taking responsibility for your life entails you making your own decisions, and accepting the outcomes. God's Word to us is that he will direct our paths if we acknowledge Him in all our ways. So, the onus lies on you to allow God to direct your path. Don't allow the spirit of indecision to rob you of God's guiding light.

3. Develop tenacity

You can only fulfill purpose and achieve possibilities with determination and persistence. Many renowned personalities in our world today who have achieved notable feats in different spheres of life all have stories of persistence before achieving those feats. Some have had to fail many times before they had their eventual breakthrough. The secret is never to give up, no matter the cost. Mistakes are bound to happen; they are all part of the learning and growth process. Never beat yourself over them, never get stuck in its claws for so long; identify the lessons learned and move on to do things better to achieve the conceived goal.

Be kind enough to yourself to always forgive yourself when you make mistakes or fall short; they are inevitable bumps along life's journey. Acknowledge your strength and weaknesses, not for fear of failure, but to know how best to harness your abilities and the opportunities that come your way to achieve your dreams. When the journey gets tough, go back to what inspired and spurred you on to go that path. Remind yourself why you're doing what you're doing. This is what will keep you right on track, even when circumstances begin to take an unfavorable turn. The "why" becomes a strong force with which you run against the wind of impossibilities.

4. Cultivate self-discipline

A life of self-disciple is key to achieving the impossible. You may think and say all the good things, but if you're not disciplined, you'll only end up living in a fool's paradise. If you sleep anytime you feel like, eat anything you feel like eating or talk anyhow, you will live a misguided and unproductive life. You have to learn to discipline your body to do profitable things, and this cuts across things you watch, listen to or engage in. One thing about our body is that it will adjust to any training we expose it to. So, learn the art of self-discipline and practice it daily.

5. Be self-motivated

You see, there is no greater joy than being your own number one cheerleader. Self-motivation is one key that will keep you moving when the odds are against you. Let's face it, your folks, friends, and people around you will not always cheer you on or motivate you towards your dream. Everyone is fighting their own demon and may not have the time to pat you in the back and push you forward. So, what do you do when motivations from people are not forthcoming? Quit? Definitely not. You have to find a way to keep yourself motivated. That is where self-motivation comes in.

I read a story on Facebook where a certain lady named Ijay recounted some challenges she encountered in the line of her job. That story is one classic example of self-motivation and I would want you to pick a thing or two from it:

"You see this lady right here, she's not about to give up on life for anything in this world. I'll tell you why. My laptop of 9 years plus was laid to rest November 2018. That laptop served me. Talk about a faithful servant. Saw me through my undergraduate and postgraduate degrees. Being a content creator and transcriber, you will agree that a laptop is a necessary tool. When it packed up, I resorted to my phone. Thank goodness I had a good phone that could do what I wanted, even though not at the same speed. I was already used to working with a laptop, and in as much as I had to make do with my available option, it was still difficult for me. There were days I end up with backaches and hand pains owing to working with my phone.

"I can't count how many times I lost enthusiasm, yet I pressed on. Of course, I have to press on and you know why? I have teens to write content for, to motivate, to inspire, and to steer in the right direction. I've got value to deliver to clients. And even though it's not always about the money, but a girl has got bills to pay. I am yet to get a new laptop, and until I get one which I don't know when (but I'm optimistic it won't be long), I'll have to keep showing up with my phone."

Why am I telling you this? This is the spirit and attitude I want you to have. No matter what it takes, don't think of quitting before the finish line. Challenges? Oh, you bet they'll come in their colors. But you, my dear, you are a warrior. You can pull through that challenge. Fight that fear, fight that discouragement; fight every ugly demon rearing up its ugly head to stop you from becoming that star in any area of your life!

Did you fall? Get back up! You are not meant to stay down. Talk to someone too. It sure helps you see possible solutions to a problem. Now, picture Jesus on the Cross. You cannot imagine the pain of each nail driven into His hands on that old rugged cross. Is it the thorny crown, or the stripes that tore His skin? Yet He endured. The Glory of redemption was far too great to give up. Was He discouraged? Sure thing! If He was discouraged, be sure you will. But, do one thing, fight till you cross the finish line. You will tell your story how you overcame, but for now, refuse to let the odds stop you. Rather, turn them to your advantage."

I think that story gave a summary of the message I want to pass across under this sub-topic. Be your own number one cheerleader. It will come in handy when others lose faith in you.

6. Develop godly confidence

As a possibility thinker and goal-getter, you cannot lack confidence in yourself and your dreams. Unfortunately, many Christians there are who suffer from a lack of confidence in themselves. The confidence I am talking about is one that is rooted in God's Word, not pride. One that is rooted in the knowledge of your identity as a child of God. Confidence that springs from your belief that you are the righteousness of God; that you can do all things through Christ that strengthens you; confidence that believes that you have an unction from the Holy One, and you know all things; that you are the head and not the tail, that, you cannot fail. Those words are not mere words; they're God's Words to you and they should form the basis of your confidence. Your confidence is not rooted in riches or natural intelligence or beauty. It is far more than that.

Your confidence is rooted in God's Word to you. He has promised to give you all that pertains to life and godliness. The word of God says while some may trust in chariots, and some in horses, we trust in the name of the Lord. We conquer through that name. The nature of God in us is not that of timidity. And so I feel sad when I see Christians timid or lacking boldness to stand before their counterparts or colleagues. We are of the lion of the tribe of Judah! Do you know what that means? It means you are meant to be bold and fearless. Your playing small does not serve God's purpose. So, do not shrink back in fear when you are up against other people. Whether it is in business, academics, marriage, profession, or whatever it may be. Be confident; your heavenly Father owns the heavens and the earth.

7. Move with people of like minds

The kind of company you keep most times rubs off on your attitude. If you must have positive results, then some things have to be done differently, and that includes the kind of company you keep. Move with people that will help you become better, not worse. Move with people that will bolster your desire to fulfill your purpose, not those that will quench it. Don't flock with a company of people that accept defeat and utter faithless and non-edifying words. Be deliberate about the kind of friends you allow into your circle. If they can't help you get better, they should not be there in the first place. Where you cannot reach by talent and dream, you can only achieve by the vehicle of people.

8. Imbibe personal principles

To live a life of purpose, there's a need to imbibe principles, beliefs, and core values that would influence your actions, decisions, and priorities. It is highly expedient to live by certain beliefs and core values, which will form the basis of what other people will know us for and how we earn their trust and respect. Paying attention to the mind of God concerning issues of life as revealed in the Bible is a great bedrock for cultivating godly principles and values. As the popular saying goes "If you do not stand for something, you will fall for anything".

Humans can be so fickle-minded, always alternating between opinions. If you let people's opinion govern you, without a principle of your own, you will end up confused and frustrated. Never be afraid to let people know the values you stand for if you intend to truly live a purposeful life. Those that fault you for being too stringent are the same persons who will praise you for your focus and singleness of purpose when your purpose begins to find expression.

9. Set your priorities right

When you're living a life of purpose, there will be activities that matter most to you which would require you to expend more of your time and effort in them. Therefore, you need to order your priorities right so that you don't dissipate your focus and energy on things that do not matter. The inability to identify the things that matter in achieving your life's goals will result in you drifting away in the torrents of life. Ecclesiastes 3:1 says that *"To everything there is a season, and a time to every purpose under the heaven"*. This verse highlights that there is a time perceived to be appropriate for every human endeavor. It is, therefore, noteworthy to understand that setting priorities with adequate attention to what is to be done in good time is vital for living a fulfilled life.

In the book entitled *"Destiny"* by T.D Jakes, one of the chapters was captioned, "Destiny Is Spelled P-R-I-O-R-I-T-I-Z-E". Here, Bishop Jakes established that investing money and resources alone will not lead to live a life of purpose if time is poorly managed or neglected. Each moment of our lives should revolve around a particular goal. Without a clear goal in mind, we tend to feel disoriented and directionless.

10. Never stop learning

Some people have a notion that the height of learning is getting to the highest educational level. But the truth is, having the highest degree in a field is not the end of learning, and learning for self-improvement is not limited to educational qualifications only. A lot of people with high educational qualifications still feel lost, depressed, and lacking in life's purpose, because they haven't found that which gives them the utmost joy and fulfillment.

Each day of our lives presents us with fresh opportunities to learn something new. There is no end to learning since the goal is to become a better version of oneself. These come with acquiring and practicing new skills, learning a new language, letting go of bad habits to adopt new, helpful habits, and exploring new opportunities. We never know what certain experiences and opportunities hold for us if we never give it a shot! The key is never to pass by an opportunity to develop, learn, and improve on who we used to be. When you commit yourself to continuous growth, an extraordinary result is non-negotiable.

11. Challenge yourself

You will never be able to live a life of purpose if you don't set yourself to do things beyond your comfort zones. As pleasant as remaining in your comfort zone may feel, the opportunities that will bring you unforgettable experiences that will lead to your fulfillment in life are in leaving your comfort zone, putting yourself up to do the very things you think you cannot do, and learn to do them. Ken Poirot once said that *"True success is achieved by stretching oneself, learning to feel comfortable being uncomfortable."* As each new experience stretches you, your capacity also increases.

12. Don't undermine your dreams

Don't ever fall for the lie that your dreams are unrealistic or not important enough for you to pursue it. Not everyone will end up on the podium or in the spotlight, we all have different places of destiny fulfillment here on earth; everyone has their place and fitting, Irrespective of what gives you joy and a sense of fulfillment, as long as you have been able to identify it and you are certain about it, then go right on to pursue it. The sooner you understand that every goal and dream you have is important and valid, the closer you will be to achieving them.

13. Live in the moment

As important as having great dreams are and having a mindset towards achieving it, it is also important to forget past failures and cherish present moments. Living in regret of the past in the present moment can hamper your zeal to pursue futuristic goals and dreams. Often, there is a tendency to drift into the past or worry about the future, but how long you are lost in them is what matters. This does not mean you should not think of future goals, but spend more time cherishing the present moment, taking actions in the present moment that will be instrumental towards achieving your future goals.

14. Break free

One of the biggest mistakes you can make in life is to allow people to dictate to you how best to live your life. Often, relatives and loved ones try to suggest to us what they think is best for us, but most times our desires and passion are not usually in line with the things that they say. The simple truth is, we are all responsible for our own lives. You are responsible for your life. When you get to a point in your life where you feel strongly that you are born to do a particular thing you truly desire and love, then, let no one keep you away from it. At other times, what will be holding you back may not be the overprotective nature and instinct of loved ones, it could be other people: a colleague, a boss in the office who is ready to give you the I-don't-think-you-are-good-enough talk.

Whatever may be the force holding you down, you should understand that the drive in you, the dream and vision you possess, that which fulfilling it will be your only satisfaction for living is a vision you carry like a woman pregnant with a child. While she travails to bring forth, she is the one to bear the pain; but the pain won't stop her from travailing until the child she is pregnant with is born. You are the one pregnant with the vision, you are the one in travail. Others do not bear the pain with you; so, let no one be responsible for your vision miscarriage.

15. Think possibilities

When you have a mindset of possibilities, you'll begin to see more opportunities in challenges instead of limitations. There is no dream or goal a man hopes to achieve that won't come with challenges seemingly big enough to deter him. But those things can only discourage, not stop you. The first book written by the renowned author, T.D Jakes, titled *Woman, Thou art Loosed!* was initially rejected by different publishers. This would have been enough to deter anyone from pushing through the idea of being an author. Later, he got an opportunity to self-publish the book, a process that would cost him $15,000. So, he had the option of either buying a house, for which he and his wife had saved up all the money they had or simply invest it into self-publishing. With the support of his wife, they both decided to invest in self-publishing their first book. It was a decision that brought them a huge turnaround. The author still has the book recorded as his highest selling book, with millions of copies already sold. Irrespective of the challenges staring us in the face, here's what our confidence should be anchored upon: "*I can do all things through Christ which strengtheneth me*" (Philippians 4:13).

Living an intentional life is not an easy task. Yet, it is achievable. All you need to do is follow the guidelines I highlighted here and commit your plans into God's hands. Surely, he will give you the grace to live a deliberate, intentional life.

7

WINNERS NEVER QUIT

"Never give up, for that is just the place and time that the tide will turn."

— Harriet Beecher Stowe

We already agree that life is full of adversities and every person who will pass through the face of this earth will go through challenges. However, already established also is that the difference between those who emerge victorious and those who fade away like vapor are those who never considered quitting in the midst of the storm.

Once again, the story of the biblical Joseph comes in handy here. No doubt, his story resonates deeply with many. They have been cast into the dungeons of failures and defeat more than they can count on their fingers, and they have made up their mind to resign to fate and pine away. Unlike this boy who persevered and held on to his dreams despite the seeming impossibility of his dreams being fulfilled, they have opted for the easiest but deadliest way out—giving up.

Quitting is not an option if you ever think of making a success out of your life. I listened to a message months ago where the preacher mentioned that there's no such thing as failure, that failure is when you refuse to pick up yourself when you fall and learn from the lessons of the mistakes you call failure. The people we look up to, who have made a name for themselves and built global relevance are who they are today because in the molding times of their lives, the times of adversity when they could have chosen to give up rather than get going, they decided to make themselves go through the fire of refining to become the shining and pure gold we love to reckon with.

While challenges and obstacles on our path in life are inevitable— only those who never try, never fail; and they eventually amount to nothing in life. Our attitude towards the experiences we have will determine the result we get in the end. Brian Tracy in his book, *No Excuses: The Power of Self-Discipline*, said, "Your ability to persist in the face of all setbacks and temporary failure is essential to success in life." This is the gospel truth you should hold on to with your right hand. Look within yourself, the times you've wanted to give up on the dreams you were pursuing, the times you've felt achieving your goals was a mirage, and the many times you've made up your mind to call it an end, were those not times you were not persistent enough? Napoleon Hill makes us understand that persistence is to the character what carbon is to steel.

RECIPES FOR SUCCESS

You can't talk about being a winner without mentioning the qualities of persistence, determination, doggedness, and resilience. If these characteristics are lacking in a man, that man will throw in the towel at the slightest challenge that comes his way. No matter how much he is motivated to hold on a little longer, there is nothing in him to sustain the motivation. Determination will make you hold on tenaciously to see the fruition of your goals. Doggedness and resilience are anchors that will hold you when the center can no longer hold, and everything you've labor for seem to crumble. How much of these qualities you've built in yourself will determine whether or not you will quit or keep standing. You'd have to be as strong as the house built on the rock so you're able to stand when the storms come. Your attitude determines your altitude, you know?

Broken crayons still color. Failure leaves us feeling broken. Constant rejection leaves us battered. Many times we're crushed under the weight of life's challenges, but does that leave us with the option of quitting? No! Why? Because broken crayons still color. Regardless of the number of times you've failed, regardless of the number of times your back gets down on the floor, regardless of the number of rejection letters you've received and the nos that will be left in your trail, the best comeback you can have is to pick yourself up over and again and come out stronger. You can't pass through failure and allow failure not to pass through you. You might want to ask, how? Failure passes through you if you go through that challenging phase and it builds in you a stronger reason never to give up if you have to ever experience such things again. It builds in you a resilient spirit that is always willing to get to the end of the road. Rather than failure serving as the rocks hurled at you to bury you, make it the stepping stones to your desired destination.

Let's look at this illustration together. Two people who have to walk through a passage which serves as the only pathway to their destination. They have no idea of what is on the way but that is the only way to attain their goal. Any other route they attempt to take will take them off the radar and they'd be completely lost. They get themselves ready and begin their journey. The passage is filled with light and it's the smoothest journey they could have ever dreamed of. As they move on, the passage begins to get dark. The farther they go, the darker it becomes. A looks B in the eye, shakes his head, and declares that he can no longer continue. "I quit," he says. "You can keep moving if you want to, but as for me, I'd rather stay here and enjoy the little success I have." He picks up his bag and turns towards the direction of the light.

B keeps moving through the dark alley. He hits his legs several times against bricks scattered around. Time and time again he made up his mind to quit moving, but he could not remain in the dark passage either. He had gone too far to look back. He picked his baggage and kept pushing through the dark and lonely passage. The darkness began to give room for the light shining from the other end of the passage. At the end of the passage were people throwing their hands in jubilation, a trophy in their hand ready to give it to the one who walked through successfully.

DETERMINE TO TRIUMPH

What do you do when the circumstances weigh you down and it looks like there's no hope for you? Do you remain at the place where it looks smooth and rosy and remain stagnant or you forge ahead through the darkness to your destination? Life is just like that passage, and the darkness symbolizes the failures, adversities, and hurdles you will have to cross. There are many, who, because they stayed on the other side of failure and crippling fear, never had their day in the sun.

If you have a dream of being successful, which I believe you have because you have this book in your hand, you're not going to be a stranger to failure; but one thing you should be a stranger to and run away from is giving up. Your name should not be once mentioned or written down in the book of records of those who cast their dreams and aspirations in the bin. It should not be said of you that in your lifetime you quit.

Do you know the antidote to quitting on your dreams? Every time you fall, pick up yourself and keep moving. If you fall again, pick up yourself, re-strategize, and do it a different way and keep moving. Don't do the same thing you did that resulted in your previous setback and expect a different result. Do things differently, for even when you do and they result in failure, you're learning different ways of how not to do things which someday will be a light bulb brightening the way of those coming behind you. Thomas Edison said, "I have not failed. I've just found 10,000 ways that won't work."

In your failure lies the ability to show those coming behind you that you have what it takes to show them the way and light their paths. You become a giant in your field rather than an insignificant player because you learned through the failures when others felt the best option was to throw a pity party for themselves and give up. Giving up drives the nail in the coffin for any endeavor you set out to achieve. What it takes not to throw in the towel is within you. Be like the righteous man who, though he falls seven times rises up again. Face that giant that wants you to cower and give up, and tell it not gloat over you, because though you have fallen, you will rise again.

I want you to know this, people may not help you rise when you're down. They may even want you to remain in a fallen state perpetually. But you're the one to remind yourself that you're a winner and you won't remain on the floor. You have to rescue yourself; you have to rise again. You must never give in to failure, never give in to defeat, never give in to rejections and never give in to disappointments. Don't be tied to what people say because you failed. They may scorn you because you're making an attempt and they may jeer at you that it will be an effort in futility, but you have to ignore their jeering. Rather, let it be the fuel that will push you to your success, and not the water that will quench your fire.

Be like the frog who kept jumping until he jumped out in the story of the two frogs. There were two frogs in the company of other frogs who fell into a pit. The two frogs attempted to jump out but the other frogs told them not to try because they were as good as dead in the pit. One gave in to their words and quit trying. He ended it in that pit. The second frog who was deaf kept jumping harder despite what the other frogs were saying until he jumped out. When he was asked if he didn't hear what they were saying, he said he was deaf and he felt they were cheering him on to jump. What can you glean from this story? Practice selective deafness. Take it that the naysayers are cheering you on to success and silence them with the results you produce. Let them turn around to sing your praise that you never gave up and you have motivated them not to give up.

Do you know the beautiful thing about not giving up? When people look at the picture of your life after you've attained the great height you struggled to get to, they do not see the failures you've left in your track, they only see the multiple success you achieved because you did not quit. Let's hear from one person who had many reasons to quit but did not. He had the attitude of I stop trying only when I get it. Albert Einstein said, "I have tried 99 times and I have failed, but on the 100th time came success. Today, he is not known as the person who failed a certain number of times, but as the person who developed the theory of relativity, one of the two pillars of modern physics. He's also known to have influenced the philosophy of science.

No Excuse for Failure

What's your excuse for wanting to call it quit on your dreams? How many times have you tried and failed that you've now issued a warrant of defeat on yourself? There are many brands you're familiar with, which you admire their achievements today because they took it upon themselves that they have only one goal in life— not to quit on their dreams and inventions.

Let's take a look at the life of someone who today is world renowned because he kept pushing through the barriers and scaling the hurdles. James Dyson is a British inventor known for the Cyclone bagless vacuum cleaner. He was frustrated with his family's vacuum and he set out to invent a better one. He borrowed capital from two people to set out on his invention. He was ousted from Kirk- Dyson because of financial friction and he left without his designs that he had come up with. Undeterred, he spent the next five years barely managing to survive while producing an almost unbelievable 5,127 prototypes until finally, the world's first bagless vacuum cleaner arrived. His invention was not accepted in the United Kingdom as it would have disturbed the valuable market for replacement dust bags. Faced with this challenge, he decided to launch his product in Japan. After his invention was rejected by the major manufacturers, he set up his own manufacturing company, Dyson Limited. His invention was eventually accepted in the United Kingdom after ten years through a television advertisement where it was emphasized that, unlike most of its rivals, the Dyson vacuum cleaner did not require the continuing purchase of replacement bags. After many years of rejections and failures, Dyson finally had his own business, manufacturing his revolutionary cleaner.

We can also draw motivation to be persistent in achieving our dreams from the lives of Masaru Ibuka and Akio Morita, the founders of Sony.

When you feel— it's a feeling and not the true state of things— remind yourself that you can do it and you don't have to chicken out. Keep going. Keep pushing. Keep moving. Even if it means crawling to the finish line, by all means, get to the finish line. That's only when you can be declared a winner. If you do not quit, for the rest of your life you'll remember you did not stop fighting to achieve your dreams and you'll be forever grateful for it, but on the other hand, you will live in the regret of ever giving up. Give it all it takes on the field of life. Don't walk out on your dreams having done less than your best.

It's good to read great stories of people who did not quit and are renowned today. It's also good to know the reasons you should not quit on anything you lay your hands on and set your heart to. However, how can you apply what you've learned. When you're faced with or before you're faced with the difficult situation that will want you to quit, what should you do?

Determine in your heart that come what may, you won't give up. You don't do the determination when you're faced with the situation. You must have done this determination long before you find yourself in that position of wanting to quit. "...and Daniel purposed in his heart..." He purposed before he was faced with the temptation, so when he was face to face with the attractive alternative, he held fast to what he had already determined in his heart. In an advert by Kanu Nwankwo, one of Africa's most decorated footballers, he said, *"...and I was determined to never give up."* Be determined.

Another thing you can do is to have an accountability partner(s). These are trusted people who will keep you accountable to your goals and when you're faint and your determination is fading away, they're right there to stoke the fire till it keeps burning again. You can't walk the road alone and expect not to get faint. Two are better than one, for when one falls the other is there to lift him up. Have people that will pick you up when you fall.

Closely related to having accountability partners is have mentors. Mentors are there to guide you. They've gone through that path you're passing through and they know how best to navigate. There's no uncharted territory, and even if there is and you're the first to tow that path, know that you have a great responsibility of leading those coming behind you and you can't afford to disappoint them.

"I have fought a good fight, I have finished my course, and I have kept the faith. Henceforth, there is laid up for me a crown of righteousness..." This was the declaration of Apostle Paul, having pushed through all the hurdles and sufferings for the sake of the faith and overcame. He was certain of the reward he had because he did not quit, he did not give up on his goal, which is the promulgation of the gospel. How does this relate to you? Declarations like this are only made by people who through the trial and challenges decide that whatever it will cost them, they will do any other thing but quit.

DARE TO WIN, BECAUSE YOU CAN!

Will you choose to quit when you know the prize ahead or will you run the race regardless of the many attractive alternatives that will want to seduce you to give up? The choice is yours. The ball is in your court and how you play it determines your outcome.

I have set before you quitting on your goals because of the failures you have experienced, and finishing strong despite the storms that rock your boat, but I'll plead with you that you should do all it takes to finish the race and finish well that you might have a testimony to share and a victory to claim.

As I conclude this chapter, let this ring in your ears and settle in your mind that footprints in the sand of time were not made by those who quit, but by those who did not give up when they had every reason to.

Winners never quit, for at the end of every tunnel you'll see the light if you do not quit. As Thomas Edison rightly said, "Many of life's failures are people who did not realize how close they were to success when they gave up… Our greatest weakness lies in giving up. The most certain way to succeed is to try just one more time."

You were born to win – and you have all it takes to do just that. So, dream, dare and determine to succeed. Yes, you can!

www.ingramcontent.com/pod-product-compliance
Lightning Source LLC
LaVergne TN
LVHW051843080426
835512LV00018B/3038